I0063778

You'll love this book if...

- It's time for you to build a compelling personal brand and take centre stage.

- You're intrigued to discover how you can become an authentic person of influence.

- Your comfort zone is in danger of holding you back.

- You recognise that it's time to step out and step up!

- You want powerful tips and templates, not marketing theory.

- You're a heart-led entrepreneur, committed to sustainability and success.

"It's one thing to start your own business but creating and developing a brand – business and personal – that resonates with your target audience and really reflects who you are, requires skill, subtlety, wisdom and courage. Dee's natural, conversational style of writing and effortless sharing of her expertise ensures the subject of branding is accessible and empowering. She helps you to get under the bonnet so that you can use all the business tools at your disposal, to create a memorable brand that packs just the right punch."

Lucy Pitts

Co-Founder and Editor of Sussex Exclusive

About the Author

Dee is a multi-award-winning Fellow of The Chartered Institute of Marketing. Only 3% of marketers worldwide are awarded Fellowship status. She is also a number one bestselling marketing author with books including *The 15 Essential Marketing Masterclasses for Your Small Business* (Wiley), rated 'an excellent read' by *The Sun* and winner of The Bookbag non-fiction book award. Her previous book, *The Ultimate Small Business Marketing Book* hit the Amazon charts at 150 before remaining a top 10 category bestseller for five years. Following this success, Dee was offered a publishing deal by CITIC Publishing in China.

Throughout a 40+ year marketing career, Dee has worked with many authentic business founders from all sectors, helping each one to build their personal brand and become a key person of influence. She has followed the same process when building her personal brand, with significant, measurable success and often, extraordinary results.

A sales-driven marketer, with an unrelenting focus on supporting small businesses, Dee has generated £12million+ sales. She's renowned for her practical approach to marketing on a shoestring and has been a keynote speaker at many national and global events.

Branding for small businesses remains a lifelong passion of Dee's, so this book was inevitable. It was simply a matter of time before she cleared the decks so she could start writing in earnest.

Other Titles by Dee Blick

Non-Fiction

*Powerful Marketing On A Shoestring Budget:
For Small Businesses*, 2008

The Ultimate Small Business Marketing Book, 2011

*The 15 Essential Marketing Masterclasses for Your Small
Business: Powerful Promotion on a Shoestring*, 2013

*The Ultimate Guide to Writing and Marketing a
Bestselling Book – on a Shoestring Budget*, 2014

Fiction

*The Boutique: 9 Gripping Powerful and
Poignant Short Stories*, 2025

YOU'RE THE
BEST!

HOW TO BUILD AN AUTHENTIC
AND MAGNETIC PERSONAL BRAND

Dee Blick FCIM

First published in Great Britain in 2025
by Book Brilliance Publishing
265A Fir Tree Road, Epsom, Surrey, KT17 3LF
+44 (0)20 8641 5090
www.bookbrilliancepublishing.com
admin@bookbrilliancepublishing.com

© Copyright Dee Blick

Author photo credit: Sophie Ward

The moral right of Dee Blick to be identified as the author
of this work has been asserted in accordance with the
Copyright, Designs and Patents Acts 1988.

All rights reserved. No part of this publication may be
reproduced, stored in a retrieval system, or transmitted,
in any form or by any means without the prior written
permission of the publisher, nor be otherwise circulated
in any form of binding or cover than that in which
it is published and without similar condition
being imposed on the subsequent purchaser.

A CIP catalogue record for this book is available
at the British Library.

ISBN 978-1-917534-07-9

Drew, for always being there and for always believing in me.

Contents

Foreword

I met Dee at a networking breakfast in 2005 and was fortunate to win a prize for one of her marketing MOTs. Dee was building her business, The Marketing Gym. Coming from a marketing background myself, I foolishly thought Dee would come along, review my marketing activities, and tell me there was little more she could add. I was wrong. It only took a few questions from her to establish that I was missing some of the most fundamental activities from my marketing programme. She quickly set about putting this right.

With my father, I'd launched our own brand of coolant leak repair to the UK automotive market a few years earlier. Business was okay, but I was new to running a business and was struggling with multiple tasks. Certain areas, such as marketing, were not receiving sufficient attention. I'd prepared a nice marketing plan but was failing to implement the basic tactical activities – the things that deliver results, rather than theory.

It was Dee who identified this and introduced several straightforward, highly effective marketing activities, which quickly delivered results. She was able to break these down into manageable tasks, which made perfect sense. The aim was to build a powerful brand that could take on and beat the established, long-standing industry names.

During this time, Dee began encouraging me to build my personal brand through many channels both in the UK and the USA. This included interviews in automotive magazines (sometimes with Dee interviewing me, which the editors appreciated!), responding to important research in the automotive aftermarket, and speaking at seminars and events, attended by technicians and motor factors, our two core target markets. I've continued with this, thanks to Dee nudging me, advising me that building my personal brand can only serve to support our bigger brand. She's right. Editors, broadcasters, and bloggers approach me for comments when they're writing about something topical within our market. Sometimes, they approach me with the latest research to ask if I'll write about it, which gives us great in-depth coverage. The same magazines have also asked me to judge competitions, provide case studies of customers, and speak at their industry events. And because we've built a good working relationship with them, they always find room for our press releases.

Dee has always been committed to building her name and reputation and even in her early years, she had a full list of clients, plus a long waiting list. I remember attending a 'Dragon's Den' style event with her, at a university business school where we were both judges. Two of the marketing consultants mentioned they were struggling to get clients. I remember thinking, 'If you can't promote your own personal brand and business successfully, how can you help clients do the same?' The brand 'Dee Blick' is a testament to Dee's skill at building her personal brand and business brand.

With Dee's help, over the years I've been able to build an exceptional brand, including what is now the number one bestselling product in its category in the USA. We've grown from six figures to several million. Along the way I've come to realise that the brand is not just the name on the box or bottle, it's the person and the people behind it. It's natural to doubt your abilities, but mastering the basics and focusing on steady progress can help you build a strong foundation for success in branding, business, and personal growth.

I'm not saying it's always easy. For me, having Dee by my side, advising, guiding, and teaching me, has made me realise I could achieve my goals. In 2005 we sold 50,000 bottles – this year we'll sell over a million. We've fought off big attacks from global corporates, had competitors trying to copy us and our brand, and weathered Covid. The common denominator throughout was the strength of the brand, the loyalty customers had to this brand and the people behind it – their personal brands.

So I strongly encourage you to read this book, and, if you haven't already, Dee's previous books. Absorb and apply her hard won, truly valuable advice, stick to your plan, and build a successful personal and business brand.

Mike Schlup
Managing Director of Kalimex

Introduction

If you're ambitious and curious, keen to explore what branding can do for you and your business, I've written this book for you.

As a marketer, specialising in working with small businesses, I know you're often strapped for time. And you can't afford to commit your precious time on marketing tactics that don't work. Where can you find marketing and branding know-how, time-served tips, and tools that are far removed from theory, and that have been proven to work, for businesses like yours? Dip into these pages for the answers. You won't be disappointed.

I also recognise that small businesses must do more than pay lip service to marketing if they're to gain a significant commercial advantage. They must be visible beyond their logo, with an authentic and magnetic brand that starts with the founder and moves seamlessly into their business. Search online for the solutions, however, and the sheer volume of information can be overwhelming and often, contradictory.

That's why I wrote *You're the Best!* My aim was to distil 40 years of working with small businesses in the fascinating area of branding and make my advice accessible, inspiring, and easy to implement. If you want to grow your personal brand for maximum impact and at minimal cost, you'll find the route map within this book, with my hand guiding you on every page.

My advice comes from the coal face of supporting small businesses for over four decades. As a marketer who walks her talk, I've followed the same process to build my personal brand, with considerable success. I've also backed up my practical experience as a Fellow of The Chartered Institute of Marketing. Only 3% of marketers worldwide are awarded Fellowship status.

Everything you read here in this book has served its apprenticeship to deliver results on a grand scale, sometimes globally, always on a lean budget. Absorb every chapter, because having the winning approach at your fingertips puts you in pole position and makes it your best business buddy.

I wish you the very best as you embark on this exciting journey, or indeed as you continue, with a comprehensive toolkit you can trust.

Dee Blick

CHAPTER 1

My Story

From the ordinary to the extraordinary

*"I did not have a
personal brand,
let alone a magnetic one.
But I wanted more."*

I was rising through the ranks as a marketing executive at a well-known, household-name company, relishing the thrill of leading high-profile campaigns that shaped the brand's story. Backed by a company that believed in my potential and invested in my growth, I found myself in a role where challenge and opportunity went hand in hand – and I loved it.

Despite feeling supported at work, a nagging voice inside my head echoed the idea that now was the moment to take time out to raise my two boys. The early morning commute and frequent overnight stays didn't fit into my new life. This time was precious to me.

After being a full-time mum for a few years, that little voice inside my head was echoing once again: *You need to grow and expand into being the Best You!* Enough was enough, so a change of direction was my pressing thought. I wanted to be in control of my destiny, what I earned, the hours I worked, and who I worked with.

The result of time spent percolating those thoughts and ideas pushed me into taking a risk, and so I launched a new business, offering marketing-on-a-shoestring services to small businesses. At first, it felt like a promising start, as I picked up a few clients who subsequently decided to keep me on a monthly retainer.

A year into my business, I had a confidence-jarring experience. The kind that stops you in your tracks and makes you question your ability. An accountant asked me to pitch for a monthly retainer service. I quoted what I thought was a reasonable day rate, only to be informed in a stinging email that as a sole trader, I was charging too much. To be retained, I had to reduce my fees.

This feedback was a blow to my confidence. The immediate impact was crushing. I'd researched the going rates and mine were well within them. Once my ego had recovered, I reflected on his email.

His perception of me had influenced my current reality. He dismissed the fact that I had a decade of marketing experience as if it didn't matter. In his eyes, I was an audacious sole trader. I didn't ever want to be in that position again, so I gave myself the challenge of moving from being the *seeker of work* to the *sought-after*. I wanted clients approaching me to be more concerned about retaining me than about my fees.

This experience made me realise I had to make my business more visible. I joined a local networking group, which helped improve my visibility. As a result, my confidence grew, as did my public speaking skills. However, I knew that if I wanted to capitalise on my skills and experience, I had to find a bigger stage.

My echoing voice challenged me once more. What would make me stand out, other than the fact that I'd taken the best assets from my previous role and repurposed them to benefit small businesses?

Right here was the wake-up call I needed.

The realisation that I didn't have a personal brand, let alone a magnetic one, hit me like a ton of bricks. How was I going to achieve more? I dug deep into my experiences to find the answer, that I had to cultivate a magnetic presence, allowing me to draw people to me. Being authentic was not a problem; I had to be more effective at conveying it.

I began thinking about public speaking at local events attended by small businesses. If I could appeal to more people by sharing my marketing expertise, this would be the first rung on the ladder to my success.

In my hometown, there was an event called Microbiz, aimed at small business owners. My initial idea was to pitch myself as a speaker, using my back story as the hook. Determination and perseverance were the key ingredients necessary to achieve success, and I delivered two talks. Afterwards, there were queues of people wanting to discuss their businesses and share their marketing challenges. I had an Oprah moment, and every person received a copy of my talk.

Shortly after this, my business began to take off. My reputation was growing as people chose to contact me after hearing good things about my work. The consequences of this newfound success meant that I could dream bigger, so I contemplated writing a book. At this point, I was writing for several magazines on behalf of clients' businesses. My reputation and business were thriving, resulting in three awards for my work, which gave me the confidence to write a book.

Not knowing much about publishing, I used a vanity publisher and my book, *Powerful Marketing on a Shoestring Budget*, was born. In the run-up to publication, I began searching for local business events and started pitching for a talk, followed by a book signing. Several bookings followed. No payment, but I could promote my book at each talk.

I also pitched a book review to the Federation of Small Business magazine, ensuring I'd contacted the reviewer beforehand so he was ready to receive it. His review was glowing. The book made it into the bestseller list and stayed there for several months.

I was now in full flow, building my reputation as a marketer, specialising in working with small businesses.

I had an incredible lucky break.

John Acton, the Executive Vice President of Geopost Group, and the Chief Marketing Officer of DPD, contacted me. He'd bought my book and wanted me to deliver a keynote talk to his team at their annual conference in London. I kept reading his email, thinking it was a mistake.

Was I daunted given this was my first paid public speaking engagement? Absolutely, but I realised it was what I needed.

I recall John, sitting in my lounge, after travelling from his base in France. I became so engrossed in conversation I forgot the pizza in the oven. Serving him a barely edible lunch is something I still cringe at. When John enquired about my speaker fee, I was at a loss for what to quote. I should have thought about this beforehand, but I'd been distracted by his imminent visit. In the end, he rounded up my suggested fee to £1,800 plus expenses. He also bought a copy of my book for every member of his team.

For my first official paid speaking engagement, this was unbelievable. I was determined to repay John's faith in me by giving it my all at his conference.

I want to share how I approached this speaking engagement and how it went on the day. If you're planning to use public speaking as a route to building your personal brand, I recommend that you approach it with the same attitude.

Because I was scheduled to speak first thing in the morning, I travelled to London the night before. Arriving early gave me the opportunity to mingle with the delegates and with John. After my talk, I stayed on so that people could chat with me in the breaks and I could sign their books. There was a real buzz around the signing and the feedback was positive. I vividly recall the speaker who followed me. He arrived a few minutes before his talk and promptly disappeared afterwards. I decided that if I were lucky enough to speak at other events, I would stay afterwards (provided the host welcomed it). I would travel to the hotel the night before, so I was ready at early doors, primed and prepped. I would also provide each attendee a professionally produced set of the marketing tips from my talk, in a branded folder. I would rather over-deliver than fall short.

Adopting this practice has resulted in me speaking at many events, where the host has been pleased to involve me in their conference. Sometimes, they've asked me to stay on and deliver a masterclass, sign books, announce the winners of a competition, be part of a judging panel or speaker forum, or to round off the event. My enthusiasm has helped me to secure repeat bookings and recommendations. I would encourage you to approach your work with great enthusiasm.

So given that I started with a mission to build a personal brand that was magnetic, what else have I done over the years in pursuit of this goal up to the present day?

What follows is a potted history of most of the strategies I've deployed all guns blazing to advance my business and, of course, my personal brand, over four decades. I started out with a handful of projects and as my confidence and experience grew, I added more until eventually, I was being approached by organisers, sponsors and journalists. The wheel had come full circle. I had become magnetic! Please don't be overwhelmed looking at this list and thinking that you need to start your brand-building journey with something similar. You don't! And neither did I.

Many of the things I share were slow-burner projects; it took a chunk of time to piece the project elements together. For example, securing a monthly column in a prestigious magazine involves many emails, online meetings and usually an initial trial to ensure that both editor and readers like your work. Whereas speaking at a small local business event usually takes up more of your courage than time. You will find your own flow and rhythm of working. Starting with a curated list is perfect. My advice is that you continue to look for opportunities. As your confidence and faith in your own abilities grows, you will notice these initiatives everywhere!

As we embark on a mission to build your personal brand, a willingness to push out of our comfort zone fires up the mind and primes us to be receptive to remarkable things that would usually pass us by. Again, this is something I share in more detail later in the book.

Start small, with a willingness to explore the opportunities that are on your doorstep before arriving at your curated list of a few projects. The rest of this book is designed to help you to do this.

As you read through the following, the brand-building benefits should become apparent, so allow your mind to wander. What appeals to you? Are there a few things you can see yourself committing to now with relative ease? Is there anything that intrigues you sufficiently to research further? Are you potentially sitting on a goldmine of an opportunity and you're fired up at the thought of it? I hope so! These are all encouraging signs that you are ready to start on your personal brand-building adventure.

My Brand Building Glossary

Magazines, Online, Printed and Blogs

I have…

- Contributed content on a broad range of topics from health and wellbeing to marketing on a shoestring, writing a book and overcoming personal challenges. This is the most powerful and effective way to showcase your influencer status and your knowledge, not least because you can promote every piece of content beyond the publication it appears in.

- Written blogs for an event organiser's social media. This worked well at The Business Show for example, where I shared marketing tips in the run-up to the event and on the day itself. If you're looking to gain the maximum exposure from speaking, this is something to be embraced, not ignored.

- Secured full-page editorial in a show magazine, again by contributing valuable content. The benefits are significant. Visitors have read about you online before attending the show, they have then read about you in the show magazine, and finally they have seen you speak. Three moments of truth that have formed a strong and enduring impression of you.

- Launched regular columns in several magazines and websites (consumer, trade, business, wellbeing), online and in print. Every month, readers tap into my tips and insights on a range of subjects. I benefit from valuable exposure at no cost. This 'frequent focus' helps establish trust with readers over time and is much more powerful than advertising. It also contributes significantly to your growing status as a person of influence.

Public Speaking From Local to National and International

I have...

- Volunteered as a backup speaker so that if a keynote speaker cancels, the organiser can ask me. This strategy worked at The Business Show (and at other events). It not only gives you additional exposure, but it also makes you even more popular with the organisers. You will usually find they are receptive when you pitch to speak again.

- Been accepted as an approved speaker for the Women's Institute, which has led to speaking opportunities and book signings. Again, by finding credible associations, you add further lustre and credibility to your personal brand.

- Spoken at local and regional book festivals, sharing my author journey. When you become part of a local event, you will also benefit from the associated PR to promote it. An online local magazine or newspaper is likely to have a reach that extends beyond the local community, giving you an even bigger audience than the actual event you're speaking at.

- Always made a point of getting to know the press team and the people who recommend, book, and handle speakers. I want to be front of mind when an opportunity arises. It takes a little time to be on first name terms with each person, but it's important to dedicate your time with a good heart, knowing the payback could be several months down the line.

- Promoted an organiser's events on my social media. When you do this, you gain extra brownie points, and it invariably opens the door to further opportunities. Organisers love speakers that share their posts and comment on them.

Events, Workshops and Book Signings

I have…

- Created author workshops on how to write and promote a non-fiction book. This is the ultimate in profiting from your passion when you're showing others how to do it.

- Created author workshops on how to write compelling characters from real-life experiences, delivered at bookshops, including Waterstones. The power in such a project lies with your co-partner and their reputation. This is why I am always open to joint ventures when I am confident about the subject matter.

- Offered a book signing at several events I have spoken at, to add a little sparkle. My philosophy is that if you don't ask, you don't get! It pays to be bold, and this action alone has boosted my book sales and helped an organiser to enhance their event. Fine-tuning your radar to look at mutually beneficial opportunities should become second nature to you.

- Held book signings at book shops including Waterstones. These events are gold dust when it comes to introducing you to a new audience of potential customers and fans, advocating for your book. And, of course, it boosts your street credibility.

- Delivered masterclasses at events organised by The Chartered Institute of Marketing. This is an example of how aligning with your professional body can leverage your personal brand because you are then seen as a credible, respected authority in your field.

- Organised several conferences and marketing masterclasses for my business, with the theme of empowering small businesses to thrive. If you can see compelling reasons to host your own events, explore with a curious mind.

Mentoring – Sharing Knowledge and Expertise

I have…

- Offered mentorship to authors, including first-time authors and successful, renowned journalists, at no charge. This usually comes when you realise that you have accrued so much know-how and experience that you must share it!

- Created free drop-in marketing clinics for small businesses. You may well find yourself offering similar no-charge support so that others can benefit from some of your expertise. It takes little from you and others can really benefit from the halo of your experience.

- Created online and in-person marketing mastermind groups for businesses that would not usually have the funds to work with an experienced marketer. Again, this can be part of your journey as a person of influence when your motive is about sharing is to help others.

- Been a judge at competitions aimed at students studying business and marketing. This not only supports local initiatives with young people in education, but it also enhances your reputation as a person of influence.

Media Including Radio, Press Events and Podcasts

I have....

- Been interviewed on many radio shows including BBC Radio Sussex and UK Health Radio, sharing my author journey, my life in recovery from alcohol addiction, promoting my non-profit charitable events and discussing marketing for small businesses. Chatting on live radio focuses the mind and it helps build your public speaking skills. It also opens you to a bigger audience.

- Been interviewed for podcasts, most recently as a woman over 60 and the lessons I have learned in life. Podcasts are so accessible and informative that you may find yourself either creating one or finding one where you can share your insights.

- Arranged media days and press events where I've met with several journalists over the course of a day or for a few hours in a bid to secure coverage for my books and promotion of me as a marketer. You will discover the power of these media events further on.

- Given copies of my books to influencers, journalists, and introducers, always targeted and with a personal message to each person. Sometimes, we must spend a little if we want to reach key people.

Self-Fulfilment… With a Touch of Whimsy

I have…

- Supported charities to raise funds and awareness, using my skills as a marketer and author. Using our name and our resources to benefit others less fortunate is the right thing to do when the cost is so minimal, namely our time and expertise.

- Sought businesspeople with complementary skills so that collectively we have organised headline grabbing initiatives for local businesses. Most recently, this has included a non-profit conference, which I share in Chapter 11. Collaborating with talented, like-minded people ignites the mind and enables us to explore our capabilities and talents more fully.

- Most recently sponsored a dog show! This was due to my love of dogs, but the organiser positioned me in the literature as a 'successful local celebrity author.' I enjoy doing things for pure enjoyment and if I can support a worthwhile cause at the same time, even better.

Everything you have just read has played a part in building my personal brand. It has taken time, of course, not to mention masses of patience, plus a willingness to pull myself up short when I started slipping back into a comfort zone. I highly recommend developing these top personal traits so you too can become successful building your personal brand.

As you would expect, I've had my share of things that didn't work out.

- The speaking engagement with a book signing that I had pinned my hopes on vanished. Then I saw it advertised with another author.

- The magazine I was confident would feature my books left my review on the cutting room floor. They did not answer my messages politely enquiring why.

- The influencer I was keen to collaborate with failed to return my calls. Their enthusiasm was clearly all for show. I subsequently learned this was an oft repeated pattern.

- The exciting project I'd planned with a colleague went cold, and I was left wondering what was wrong with me, rather than just accepting it had nothing to do with me.

Not everything will work out, despite your passion and commitment, not to mention your desire to do the right thing. However, if you persist with a willingness to share and do something amazing that advances your brand-building cause, the positives will outweigh the negatives by a mile.

Avoid the Hard Sell Pitch When Speaking

I want to return briefly to sharing my approach when I'm offered a speaking engagement. It's easy to adopt, with authenticity at its heart.

In the thirty minutes before my first speaking engagement at The Business Show, I sat in the audience, watching the speaker, a business coach. She shared a few tips and then proceeded to inform the audience about her mastermind weekend and the cost of attending. This pitch assumed the rest of her talk.

She overran by 10 minutes, despite the organisers making it clear to us in the pre-show speaker briefing that we were not allowed to pitch, and we had to finish on time.

When I took to the stage, I made a point of telling the audience that I would not be pitching my services. They could relax.

Unbeknownst to me, the managing director of an office supplies brand was in the audience. He'd travelled from Sheffield to London to see me in action. Afterwards, Steve asked if I would speak at his company's annual conference. He went on to retain my services as a marketing mentor. I worked with the business for three years and spoke at two of their conferences. All this from just one talk.

Sharing marketing tips with my audience has served me well throughout my career. I know from chatting to other speakers that my speaker fees are competitive. Usually a book signing follows, and all my expenses are covered.

Don't use the space you're given to pitch. There's time for this afterwards when you're chatting with people who are interested in discovering more about what you offer. Be memorable for the right reasons, and your willingness to inspire your audience will pay you back.

How Writing Books Has Built My Brand

I didn't write books with making money as the main goal. Money is essential, but my focus has always been on writing the best book I could at that point in time. I also made the decision not to overpromote my books to any audience, after another speaker, also an author, had influenced me. He was billed to deliver a talk on his blueprint for building a successful business, during which he held onto his book throughout. The message he kept on repeating was that if the audience wanted to know the secrets of his success, they had to buy his book. I found his technique irritating. He would start by sharing a helpful business tip. When you thought he was going to share something profound, he would stop abruptly, saying, 'If you want to know more, you'll have to buy my book.'

After he'd said this several times, I'd heard enough. And I was not going to buy his book. I learned nothing that day, except that it reinforced what I'd already committed to doing – delivering robust marketing content to my audience, right up to the closing minutes. I've never had a person say they weren't going to buy my book because I had overshared. I have, however, attended talks where the speaker has been so intent on selling their services, including the book, that it has left audience members disgruntled.

Do the opposite! Better to share too much of your secret sauce, than not enough. You don't have to be delivering a talk or promoting a book to adopt this approach. If you can share first-class content with your target audience, focus on this to the exclusion of anything else. Your generosity will pay you back, just as it has me.

How One Book Changed Everything

Writing bestselling books has played a significant role in establishing my personal brand and advancing my career. Earlier in the chapter, I spoke about my first book. I was pleased I'd managed to take some of my marketing know-how and repurpose it into a book. However, the L plates were still on the cover. How could I, as a marketer, one of thousands, possibly claim my expertise in a book, especially when I viewed it as common sense?

A search on Amazon revealed thousands of marketing books for small businesses. This fact alone kept me cautious. My book sold around 5,000 copies which is good going for a first book, but I knew I had not exhausted my subject. Probably because it was my first book. I was pleased that the feedback was mostly positive.

When I wrote *The Ultimate Small Business Marketing Book*, my confidence levels had increased. I decided to marshal all my resources in this book. I included examples of my most successful work and didn't hold back on sharing my marketing expertise. Readers could not only learn how I approached marketing on a shoestring, but they could also see samples of my most successful sales letters, for example. I repeated this approach of sharing my work in most chapters.

It was a strategy that paid off.

After my professional body, The Chartered Institute of Marketing, made it their book of the month, it reached a position of 150 on Amazon. It stayed in the top 10 bestselling marketing books for five years. Without a doubt, it boosted my personal brand. As you can tell, being an author reaps bountiful rewards.

Speaking opportunities and offers to write in publications and blogs came flooding in. Readers, primarily small business owners, approached me, asking if I would help promote their businesses.

With book sales in the thousands, a publishing group in China approached me. They paid for the rights to translate *The Ultimate Small Business Marketing Book* into Chinese.

My professional body, CIM, then recommended me to Wiley, a UK publisher. Before I knew it, I signed a contract to write another marketing book. *The 15 Essential Marketing Masterclasses for Your Small Business* followed. This book also became a number one bestseller, selling thousands of copies. CIM promoted the book heavily, which helped enormously in establishing my status as a person of influence – a significant aspect of positioning yourself as the expert in your field.

The cumulative effect of these books meant that I didn't have to look for work. Clients found me.

Underpinning this success has been a commitment to sharing my knowledge and expertise. This trait has been the core of my authentic personal brand. Little has changed today. I now write for several publications and have embarked on public speaking once again to promote my first fiction book and this book you are reading. I have no problem, however, in saying no to something when it conflicts with my values or I can't do the subject matter justice.

Self-care is a crucial aspect of personal brand building, so be sure to look after yourself and conserve your energy for activities that will advance your cause. Remember that, like me, you can be perfectly imperfect and accomplish some truly extraordinary things. Sometimes, it can take a negative experience to give us that fire and determination; other times, we recognise the gift of being in the right place when the right things happen.

Your Takeaways

1. Regardless of the platform, share your knowledge and expertise, holding little back.

2. Can you work with your professional body to share your expertise through their learning and development programmes?

3. When something is presented to you that will help advance your personal brand, take it and work out the 'how' later.

4. Orchestrate your own brand-building opportunities. You don't have to wait for the right thing to happen.

5. Is there a book in you? If you're curious, explore the idea with an open mind.

6. If an opportunity aligns with your values, it's a sign you should say yes. Be bold and fearless, even when you feel anything but.

7. Don't worry when opportunities fail to materialise. Better ones are on the horizon.

CHAPTER 2

Kirstie's Story

It's your time to shine!

"Are you guilty of loving your business, but failing to align your personal brand with it?"

A conversation over coffee with Kirstie Betts, the co-founder of Pied A Terre Adventures (PATA), inspired this chapter.

PATA is an award-winning walking and outdoor travel company. Based in Horsham, they lead walking adventures with qualified guides throughout the UK and overseas.

I've known Kirstie for several years. She's a warm and friendly woman, with a back story before PATA as an occupational therapist and counsellor. She also volunteers for The Samaritans. As you can imagine, she's a good listener. Her son, Harvey, a fire fighter, spoke at one of my book launches, when he was just 11 years old. He had a real impact on the audience; a young, confident, and smiling boy, talking about me as an author, his parents, Kirstie and Richard, looking on proudly.

Apart from bumping into one another at local networking events, Kirstie and I have never had a proper chat. So when she messaged me to suggest a coffee catch up after her holiday, I jumped at the chance, certain that her story would make it into this book.

The message she'd shared with me on social media about her holiday was intriguing. With Richard, she had embarked on a 14-day adventure, chasing and documenting tornadoes and extreme weather. It was a holiday that was taking in Canada and America, up to the border of Mexico. Two weeks of storm chasing, with disappointment when they subsided.

This was the last thing I expected of Kirstie. Then again, she is the co-founder of a business that's all about putting the adventure into team building and holidays.

When we met, I wanted to know more about her adventurous streak. She told me that from an early age, she loved sitting alone in the family garden, surrounded by rain, hail and thunderstorms. Any spell of severe weather and out she went, her parents unaware. She knew what their answer was likely to be. She spoke of feeling alone, that she could not find another soul that also loved extreme weather. Happily, she met Richard and was thrilled to discover he was cut from the same cloth. They both shared a passion for chasing extreme weather. Their subsequent holidays were all about walking adventures and dramatic weather seeking.

During our conversation, Kirstie showed me several striking photographs of tornadoes she had captured. She spoke with such fire and passion that I decided not to talk about my imminent holiday in Devon, where the biggest risks were likely to be navigating cows and slithering in slurry.

Kirstie told me that on these adventure holidays, she would keep a daily journal to look back on, rather than to share with an audience. She had not considered the latter.

I put my branding hat on, because there was a pressing question I had to ask her.

Given she was now taking responsibility for growing PATA (Richard is still Lead Guide but he's also involved in their other business, Trig Point Consulting), why had she not shared this side of her character to people that would be interested? I was thinking of relevant media, potential clients, key people that could introduce her business to their followers. If anyone was an example of living their brand authentically and loving their brand, it was Kirstie. Had she shared a smattering of this, with a view to promoting PATA?

She struggled to answer. Eventually, she shared that she found it hard to promote herself, but she was aware that she had to change and embrace the personal brand she had been building intuitively since childhood. It had not occurred to her that her enduring love of real outdoor adventures, from being a little girl to the present day, was compelling and entirely relevant to the big picture, the PATA story. Yet nobody outside of their family was aware of this.

In this matter, Kirstie is not alone.

Like many business owners, she had not joined the dots up, aligning the importance of her personal brand with her business brand. Yet here she was, with a golden nugget in her hands.

We discussed her journals and how they would make for interesting and unique content, shared through several channels, including Substack, the travel section of a regional magazine, and social media. Similarly, Kirstie's love of adventure had to be shared on the PATA website, in company presentations, videos and more.

The cumulative effect of this activity would be to increase interest in Kirstie, as well as in her business. Not only does she carry the message, but she also lives it.

It's not earth-shattering to say that if prospects are curious about your story, they're more likely to be interested in buying from you. Getting their attention at an early stage is essential. Your story keeps them close to your brand as you build on the next steps.

Kirstie had to take one crucial step to live her personal brand and love it. She had to start promoting herself. If anyone had the power to be authentic and magnetic, it was Kirstie.

Kirstie had not considered any of these points until we spoke. She had become so focused on pitching for business and answering enquiries that looking at the bigger picture had eluded her. However, after our impromptu marketing chat, she now had a promising idea of how she could make PATA stand out as an exciting brand, with its roots steeped in the characters and history of both founders.

As you read Kirstie's story, has any of it resonated with you?

Are you guilty of loving your business but failing to align your personal brand with it?

Have you considered how to incorporate your personal story into your business narrative to enhance its impact and relevance? And make it more inspiring?

The chapters that follow will help you to build on what's already within you, but that you're not taking full advantage of.

I would hazard a guess that you can create something truly extraordinary.

It's time to step onto that road less travelled.

Your Takeaways

1. Have you stopped to consider the power of connecting with your personal brand story? Is it time to sit down, reflect on it and write it?

2. How could your personal brand story positively impact your business story?

3. Where can you bring this story into your business to make your messages more relevant and compelling?

CHAPTER 3

Branding Your Business

**Aligning your business brand
with your personal brand**

"... the alluring pull of your brand rests on what customers think about it. And what they think about you, the ultimate ambassador for your brand."

In a world where artificial intelligence is unrelenting, having an authentic and magnetic personal brand has never been more important. It helps you stand out for the right reasons: as an exceptional, talented, and capable individual whom people gravitate towards. A person they can admire, work with, and recommend with ease.

Building your personal brand and your business brand should happen simultaneously, in harmony. As a person moves from you and into your business, they should experience the same positive feelings.

There should be no disconnect; instead, there should be one seamless flow.

Commit to the dual cause: an authentic and magnetic personal brand plus an authentic and magnetic business brand, and you will bring many people into your circle. Customers, influencers, introducers, journalists, advocates, members, and more. This has certainly been my story and that of the many clients I have worked with from all sectors.

Why are they making a beeline for you, then your business?

You've demonstrated through many channels that you're a credible and trustworthy pair of hands. People know they can count on you to deliver to the highest standards, consistently. Moreover, they don't want to miss out by not connecting with you. You have intrigued them.

Because of what a person has read about you or heard about you, they are drawn to you, confident you meet their needs. Don't be surprised that some people are not only primed and prepared, but they're also excited at the prospect of collaborating with you. With a few brush strokes, you've moved a prospect swiftly along the road to buying from you. Some will go on to become raving fans.

If you already have a healthy business brand, read this chapter to see if there are further tips you can use. If you're still at the brand-building stage or find it challenging to integrate your business into the subject of branding, I hope my practical approach appeals.

Branding for small businesses is a lifelong passion. This process began early in my career and led to the development of a branding workshop, which I have presented to thousands of delegates. This chapter is based on that workshop. I've used it to help small businesses take on the task of branding their business, with confidence, on a lean budget. It extends beyond the usual subjects of logo design and marketing communications.

Before lifting the lid on branding, I want to share a marketing tool that I use without exception for clients. Pay close attention to it because it can close the gap between a person expressing interest in your products and services, to becoming a paid-up customer.

This must be the focus for any business owner – new customers coming through the door, thick and fast, spending less time deliberating over whether to use you or not. The stronger your business brand and, of course, your personal brand, the easier it is for customers to say yes.

The Continuum of Behaviour

I refer to this as the most powerful marketing tool, ever!

The Continuum of Behaviour describes the decision-making process a person follows before they decide to buy from you or recommend you.

This process is followed regardless of whether they're existing customers, lapsed customers, cold prospects, warm prospects, influencers, potential members, supporters, or introducers.

The five steps of the Continuum of Behaviour are Awareness, Interest, Evaluation, Desire and Action.

A_____I_____E_____D_____A

How Does the Continuum of Behaviour Work?

People rarely make the decision to do business with you, or commit to supporting you, at the first touchpoint. Research shows that a person must be drip fed sufficient information about what you offer before they arrive at the decision to buy.

There's always an element of risk involved in buying from a business, or giving it a vote of confidence, by recommending it to others.

A prospect, customer, introducer, or influencer progresses through four stages before reaching the action point, where they close the deal or recommend you. And this takes time. How much time depends on several factors. This includes the financial outlay, the level of risk attached to the purchase, the number of people involved in the decision to buy, and competitors hovering close by.

In most cases, if you attempt to accelerate a person along the Continuum of Behaviour, from having no awareness of you or your business to being a fully paid-up customer or introducer, with just one communication, you're unlikely to succeed. You're asking for too much, given the lack of a relationship and the limited understanding of how the person or business arrives at the decision to buy or recommend. Trying to rush them along the continuum builds mistrust. You risk appearing unprofessional, even desperate.

If, however, your focus has been on building an authentic and magnetic personal brand, running parallel to your business brand, you'll find that when a person enquires about what you offer, they're already at the stage of being interested. They may even be at the evaluation stage and all that remains is for you to meet, to confirm their hunch that you are The One. They know about you; they like you and they've already stepped into the arena of trusting you, based on their perception of your personal brand and your business brand.

When you're next planning a marketing campaign, use the Continuum of Behaviour to plot the point at which you find your prospect, customer, or introducer, so that you can plan the next stages. Your subsequent marketing messages will have more impact because they will be accurate and targeted. Don't be tempted to carry the same message at every stage of the continuum. Messages must change, even if change is subtle.

Most of the founders I've worked with over the last 40 years have brought me into their business to look at how I can improve their prospecting success. They want more high value customers, in the shortest period possible. And they don't want to spend money on expensive, potentially hit and miss marketing campaigns. I whip out that continuum so we can begin plotting in earnest.

I also analyse the profile of the business founder so I can see the steps they've taken to build an authentic and magnetic personal brand, before determining next steps. I usually discover the need to strengthen the magnetic part. Business owners do not have a problem with being authentic. However, they will acknowledge the need to build on their public profile.

I then undertake a brand audit of their business, usually blended in with their marketing strategy. Given the business founder is often the face of the business, being authentic as well as magnetic is not just a nice to have, it's a necessity. When I explain the importance of a strong personal brand in compressing the decision-making process, I usually secure their buy in and we embark on an exciting journey together, full of promise for what we can accomplish.

It's All About *the* Brand

I hope you're convinced about the importance of brand building across the board. Because it starts with you.

Let me take you on a branding journey, so you can understand what a brand is and what it takes to build a successful business brand as well as a strong personal brand.

Because the two are intertwined.

When you get it right – an authentic and magnetic personal brand, plus an authentic and magnetic business brand – the magic really happens. As I mentioned previously, you become the *sought after*, not the *seeker*, and business profitability increases.

What Does 'Brand' Actually Mean?

Occasionally, I hear a business owner saying, 'I've got my brand sorted out.' What they're referring to is the design of their logo and how it cascades across their communications.

Philip Kotler is a marketing author, consultant, and professor emeritus. I love his description of a brand in his book, *Ingredient Branding*.

"A brand is a promise to your customers, the totality of perceptions about a product, service or business, the relationship customers have with it based on past experiences, present associations and future expectations ... brand reality is always defined by the customer's view."

Fundamentally, Kotler is saying that the alluring appeal of your brand rests on what your customers think about it. And by inference, what they think about you, the ultimate ambassador for your brand.

Pause for a moment and consider the small businesses in your community that resonate with you, the ones you gravitate towards and feel comfortable recommending. I'm sure that your thoughts on the founder play a big part in what you think and feel about their business, and how much you want to use them or recommend them. Underpinning this is the sense of ease and comfort, not to mention confidence you also feel about their actual business.

A Brand, Not Just a Business

In a sea of businesses not dissimilar to yours, a great reputation helps you stand out. Satisfying customers' needs and delivering a brilliant service are the building blocks of a strong brand. And with a strong brand, your business benefits as follows:

- Customers reward you with their loyalty even when tested by competitors. And they recommend you.

- Customers are willing to pay a higher price. The added value you offer justifies it.

- Customers are not overly sensitive about price increases. Price is important but not a deal breaker.

- You close sales more quickly. Because customers are confident in you and your business brand, it takes less time to say yes.

- Customers award you a larger share of their available spend, especially when the good times are rolling.

- When times are tough, customers are reluctant to stop using you, especially if you make it easy for them to stay.

Building Your Business into a Brand

There are five areas to focus on:

Visibility. This is what customers see when they look at your business. Visibility is the station many business owners stop at, and they stay stopped at. It's important because it encompasses your business name, logo, and associated imagery. It also includes the voice you use to communicate through words what your brand stands for, including your voice on social media. It extends to how you present yourself when promoting your business – what you look like and what you sound like, if you're on-brand, or if you're putting barriers in the way because you're standing out for the wrong reasons.

Consistency. This is about the service you deliver to customers and if it is dependable all the time. Consistency fits into the Lean philosophy of 'Right First Time on Time Every Time'. It doesn't work if on some days you go all out to deliver a sterling service, but on others, you struggle to offer the basics. Customers will not trust you and when you break their trust, all bets are off. Loyal customers become ripe for defection and prospects drift away. It will not work either if you follow your attentive onboarding of a new customer with a lacklustre approach.

Clarity. This is about the messages customers receive about your business and if they are easy to understand, relevant and compelling. If you're unable to present your business with pinpoint clarity, you create confusion in the communication channels. You make it hard for people to recommend you or talk to others in their decision-making unit. If, however, people can grasp what you offer and why it meets their needs, you're paving the way for new customers and repeat purchases from existing customers. Clarity entails paring everything down to ease of understanding.

Sustainability. This is about the important social and environmental messages that customers are looking for. Today, every business must demonstrate a commitment to sustainability. This entails putting every aspect of your business under the microscope and identifying how you can become genuinely sustainable. Statements on your website count for little if they're not backed by genuine action.

Continuity. This is about customers feeling reassured that they can trust you, that your business has roots and you're not going anywhere anytime soon. For low-price, one-off purchases, continuity is not a deal breaker, but for most businesses, customers are looking for the signs that you're in it for the long haul.

Let's look at each one of these in more detail.

Visibility

At some stage, a business will review the image they present to the full sweep of their audiences, from prospects to introducers. Over time, they become aware of shortcomings in:

- Their logo

- The typeface and style of their business name

- Any supporting images

- Their strapline

Usually, a business is established on a small budget, with design work either overseen in-house or passed to a printer, often with negligible design skills. Although acceptable when the business was new, the homespun look eventually counts against them. A professional designer may have been used at the initial stages, but the design no longer accurately reflects the business.

If you're considering rebranding your business, ensure you're involved in the design process. With no guidance, your designer may create something that does not align with your values and market position.

Create a design brief that you're both happy with.

It should include the following:

- **Are you looking for a new look or to improve on what you already have?** When one of my clients, a chartered accountant, was embarking on the design process, they didn't want to abdicate their logo, a wren. They wanted it updated and modernised to reflect their growth and expertise.

- **Your budget may not extend to an image overhaul**, but don't let that stop you from consulting with a designer about enhancing your logo and overall look. Subtle design tweaks can enhance the perception of your business. Remember, brand reality is determined by what people think about your business, so make sure yours is fresh and relevant.

- **What are the keywords that define your business?** What are the values that you live by and that underpin your offering? Include these in your design brief to paint a detailed picture that will inspire your designer. One value, one keyword, may be enough to create something spectacular.

- **Make a list of everything affected by a rebrand.** You can then decide whether you want to completely change your look or improve on what already exists.

Your designer must have this list if their design is to work effectively across every communication.

• **Do you want to change your strapline or add one?** A brilliant strapline helps you stand out from competitors who rely on their business name alone to convey what they do. A business name with no clear purpose can be at a disadvantage without the inclusion of a strapline. Here's a selection I like from small businesses, each one headed up by an authentic and magnetic leader.

'Love Water. Love Life!'
Nick Swan. Founder, Love Water.

When you meet Nick, it's abundantly clear he embodies his brand. He exudes vitality, good living, and positive energy. This strapline connects the benefits of drinking water, supplied by Nick's business, with the concept of living well and loving life. And of course, it plays to his business name.

'Enabling employers to understand mental health.'
David Beeney. Founder, Breaking the Silence.

This is a clever strapline, because in six words, David tells you what he does, the people he works with and how they benefit from using him.

'Liquid Tools.'

Gilbert Groot. Founder, JLM Lubricants, a global premium additives manufacturer, selling primarily to automotive workshops.

It's clever how just two words encompass the benefit of JLM Lubricants' products to the professional automotive technician. It also sets their products apart from cheap additives on sale in the supermarket. And it travels well in translation across the 40+ countries where the brand has a footprint.

'The go-to guide for you and your child.'

Freddie St George. Managing Director, Raring2go! A 'what's on' resource for families, available online and in print.

This clever strapline makes clear the compelling benefit of the magazines and websites to both target audiences: parent and child. Once you've read it, you understand the business name.

'From clicks to conversions, we drive your social success.'

Michelle Betts. Founder, ByJove Media.

I don't have to tell you what Michelle does! Her strapline says it all, made even more memorable with alliteration. She also conveys the compelling benefit clients derive when choosing her.

'Creative design from every angle.'
Melanie Tilly. Founder, Mel Design 360.

I like how Melanie uses the word 'angle' to align with her business name. Although her business name tells you immediately what she does, her strapline builds on this.

'The Disruptive Copywriter.'
Lucy Pitts. Founder, Strood Copywriting.

I like how Lucy's strapline arouses intrigue and curiosity. She's also ensuring her business stands out from other copywriters, with a hint of menace and excitement.

I singled out these straplines because they're simple, memorable and they support the business names. When it comes to yours, use customer-friendly language and avoid the clichéd tropes you see on the side of vans; usually a nondescript line about offering 'the best service ever.' Make yours relevant to your core business offering, including a dominant benefit.

When you start collaborating with a designer, treat them with respect. Give them everything they need to work their magic on the visual brand aspect of your business. Brilliant design can be instrumental in boosting your bottom line and enhancing what people think about your business. It's also an integral part of building your business into an authentic and magnetic brand.

Let's turn now to the voice of your business and how this shapes the perception of your brand. Is your brand voice quirky, funny, serious, stable, or disruptive? It may be a heady mix. For example, my client, Architectural Plants, specialise in designing the most exquisite gardens, using full-size trees and shrubs, grown on their 32-acre nursery in Sussex. Their brand is all about quality, innovation and sustainability. They use a quirky voice, however, to communicate what they offer, encouraging intrepid plant hunters to get in touch and start their plant hunting adventure, amongst their acreage of magnificent trees and plants. This light touch sits well alongside their offering. It adds up to making their brand memorable, friendly, and approachable.

Think for a moment about the voice of your brand. You have one but is it visible? Are you playing to its strengths, or has it become submerged underneath your growing business? Should you refine it for more impact?

As a point of inspiration, can you align your business voice to a person you know, or a character in the media, even a book, or your favourite meal? Can you paint a picture in a few sentences, not dissimilar to the profile descriptions on dating apps? Can you assign a colour to it?

These simple tasks will help you to address an important subject with ease. Then, inspiration task completed, write a short paragraph describing the voice of your brand.

I would like you to consider the voice you use on social media. It does not matter if you have separate business pages as well as personal pages. Across the board, your voice must be professional, warm, and welcoming. Potential customers and introducers will not differentiate between personal and business. If you've fallen into the trap of using your social profiles to relax so much that you've blurred the boundaries, you risk damaging your personal brand and your business brand. And if you post regularly, you must expect customers and prospects to contact you. They will expect a timely response. Being professional, accessible, and responsive is important if you want to show up socially and use your platform to build relationships. Bring your social profiles into the branding mix and use private messages to take complaints or potential controversy away from the public glare.

The second element of building an authentic and magnetic business brand is:

Consistency

Most of us are creatures of habit.

We find the businesses we like and stick with them, even when we add more into the mix. We know what to expect, which reduces or removes any perceived risk. Businesses that become successful brands understand the importance of delivering a consistent and positive customer experience. They make it their mission to ensure customers enjoy interacting with them every time they try, buy, or simply enquire.

There are brands that deliver at the lowest price point. They expect customers to lower their expectations, in exchange for paying the lowest price. But most of the time, customers want it all: a fair price, great service, and value.

How Can You Build Consistency in Your Business?

Identify every customer touchpoint, including social media. How does your business perform at each one? My experience is that businesses focus their energy and commitment on recruiting new customers, before moving swiftly to the delivery stage. Aftersales support can be lacking because the spotlight has failed to reach this part of the business, so we see inconsistencies creeping in and undermining customer confidence. You may find this exercise reveals that your business over-delivers in some areas, under-delivers in others.

Are there inconsistencies in the quality of the service customers receive? When you're busy, do service levels sink? Do you fail to answer questions on social media because you visit your pages sporadically or you've abdicated to a third party? Do you leave customer emails languishing in your mailbox when stressed? Customers will defect if this happens too often. Put your customer touch points under the microscope. At each point, do you really deliver to a consistently high standard? Implement improvements without haste.

By striving for elevated levels of consistency in your customer experience, you're moving your business closer to becoming an authentic and magnetic brand.

Sometimes, your commitment to supporting customers, through the automatic habit of over-delivering, pays you back unexpectedly.

AJ Fleetcare is a garage, based in Leeds, founded by married couple Alan and Jeanette Landale. I have mentored them for several years and have always been astonished at their attitude to customer care. Their values of consistently over-delivering for customers shone like a beacon recently. It also led to them winning a national award from the Motor Ombudsman Bureau.

In the words of Jeanette Landale:

"A new customer brought their car in for an urgent repair. He needed it to visit his dad, who has dementia and is on medication, which he'd run out of. We couldn't repair his car immediately so we told him to leave it with us, and we paid for a taxi so he could get to his dad, with the medication, on time. Later that day, he returned to collect his car. We left a little gift for his dad on the passenger seat – a box of chocolates and a card for our customer. We know what he's going through because we're also looking after a family member with dementia. Well, he only went and wrote a glowing review to the Motor Ombudsman Bureau. We were then entered into a best customer service award and out of 3,500 garages, we were voted the winner. The judges said we went over and beyond with our customer service. But this is what we do, and we would do the same thing again. We had an all-expenses-paid trip to the Houses of Parliament to be presented with the award. Then it was back to work, doing what we do best: fixing customers' cars and ensuring they leave happy and smiling."

Being a Consistent and Considerate Employer

Successful businesses become successful brands from the inside. And it starts with you as the figurehead of your business.

Every person that joins your business should understand your customer service philosophy, your values, and how you embed these values in your business.

Your onboarding should extend to showing a recruit how their role fits in with the business, and the part they play in building customer relationships. Make sure you identify any of their immediate training needs. Allowing a new person to talk to customers and handle enquiries from prospects without proper training can damage your brand. Remember, brand reality is defined by the customer's view.

Let's look at the third element of building a successful brand:

Clarity

Successful businesses that focus on brand building deliver clear, simple messages – online, at networking events, or through the printed word – at every touchpoint.

What would you say to the following questions?

1. What is our business story? Has it changed over the years, and if so, how?

2. What are our values? Are we living these values?

3. Is our focus on simplicity, or are we overcomplicating what we offer from the customer's viewpoint?

Your story is what drove you to launch your business. Told with purpose and passion, it is unique and interesting. It humanises your brand.

Many successful brands embrace storytelling. The next time you visit the website of one, search for their story.

Many speakers will start their talk with a glimpse into their early years. They will explain how they started with little more than a desire to accomplish something extraordinary. If told with humility and honesty, their story will inspire you. If you watch *Dragons' Den*, you can see storytelling in full flow. The businesses that chip away at the barriers surrounding the dragons tell a captivating story before moving onto their products or services. Their story provides that all-important context, their 'why' in action.

Have you told your story? A narrative covering your journey can be compelling. You don't have to load it with detail. Give people a window to look at your business and how it evolved from an initial idea. Two hundred words is perfect. Craft it carefully so it is authentic and appealing. Share it with your team and weave it into your communications.

As we turn to your values, I want to share a snippet of conversation showing values in action.

"My values are about being inclusive, welcoming, and empowering ... the combative manner of the trainer, including the sarcastic tone of her emails when I made a small spelling mistake, meant we could not take her beyond the initial trial session. She has no self-awareness and believes her abrupt manner is a sign of being powerful. I saw it as lacking emotional intelligence and empathy."

A friend told me this when I asked how she was getting on with recruiting new trainers. We had never talked about values before, but it was clear she knew hers.

If I asked you to share your values in a few sentences, what would you say? These values are at the heart of your business. They underpin the reasons why you want to be heard, seen and remembered. Share them in your communications. I've seen blue-chip brands run advertising campaigns on their values alone. Your values paint a picture of what drives your business.

Finally, if you want accurate answers to question three, talk to your customers and prospects, asking open questions. Explaining your services simply is an art, something you underestimate at your peril. Some businesses write their communications in an echo chamber. Not every customer or prospect will tell you they struggled to decipher your content. They'll walk away or simply restrict what they buy based on what they understand.

Once again, if customers define brand reality, yours must be able to grasp what you offer, with a clear explanation of the benefits. Use the task of revisiting your communications, through the lens of clarity, as an opportunity to make your messages more appealing and relevant. Then update each one with a sense of urgency and purpose.

Let's look at the penultimate part of the brand-building process.

Sustainability

Increasingly, businesses are looking to reduce their impact on the environment. In the automotive aftermarket where I've helped businesses evolve into trusted brands, there has been a rise in the 'Products over Parts' and 'Repair over Replace' movement. This stems from the concept that if workshops are using fewer parts and are repairing cars over replacing them, the planet benefits at both ends of the spectrum – from conserving resources, to slowing down the volume of vehicle scrappage. For one brand, JLM Lubricants, we took these two complementary trends and ran multiple campaigns, aligning their automotive additives to the central premise of each one. This led to the creation of JLM Lubricants' strapline, 'Liquid Tools.' If a workshop can use a premium additive over a product part, and as a repair over a replacement part, they are acting in a sustainable manner. JLM Lubricants are now positioned as a trade-trusted brand, supporting workshops with their premium quality additives, which work first time and that reduce a workshop's reliance on car parts.

How are you delivering your services and products to lessen their impact on the environment? And are you going above and beyond to support local or national charitable causes? Are you promoting this or keeping it to yourself?

Customers are looking for answers. Sustainability is on their radar.

Put your commitment to sustainability in writing and use it as part of your marketing communications toolkit, adding it to your website and social profiles. This will help you stand out from competitors.

And unlike JLM Lubricants, you don't have to be a global brand.

Take Katie Wellman, founder of Make Room to Breathe. She offers a professional decluttering service. If you find any space in your home overwhelming, Katie will help you to shed the 'stuff' that's holding you back, mentally and physically. I used her to reorganise a bedroom, followed by the kitchen. I was really impressed with her approach to sustainability. She takes everything away that you no longer need. We're talking old dishcloths, bits of tangled string and ribbons, plus the bigger stuff. She then sorts through every item so that she can deliver it to its rightful recycling home. Finally, the good quality items are donated to charity. Nothing Katie takes away in her car, full of the spoils from a session, goes to landfill.

When I asked Katie why she was not promoting this aspect of her service, she told me it had never occurred to her. Yet this really made her stand out. It was testament to her authenticity and commitment to running a sustainable business. She has since corrected this oversight.

We should all be more like Katie in our businesses.

Here are two businesses that stand out for their genuine enthusiasm to raise money and support charitable causes.

Founded by Peter Sutton in 1993, PMW is a full-service marketing agency with a long and impressive history of consistently raising money for local causes. To celebrate their 30th anniversary in 2023, the team put their heft behind the DO30 campaign, inviting local worthy causes to be one of 30 that would benefit from their help. The fundraising momentum has continued to the present day, earning the business a third sector award. However, proving that charity really does begin at home, in 2024 and 2025, PMW was named on *The Sunday Times Best Places to Work* list. Because employees love their place of work, with its inclusive and supportive culture, they have bought into Peter's desire to shine the spotlight on worthwhile, often under-represented local causes. Doing the right thing, sometimes without an audience watching, has played a big part in building Peter's personal brand. He was keen to instil this in his team.

Freddie St George MBE is the managing director of Raring2go! He is another modern-day philanthropist, having raised a cool £3.1 million for children's charities through his love of Minis, combined with his proud Italian heritage. His desire to fundraise, without recognition and simply by doing the right thing, aligns with the support he offers to his franchisees. Every person in his network has an equal voice, with the franchisee council he established a testament to this. Like Peter, Freddie loves fundraising and his MBE for charitable work speaks louder than his innate modesty.

Not every business has the reach or resources of Peter and Freddie, but we can all do something. For example, I'm an ambassador for a local charity, Ten Little Toes Baby Bank. As part of my support, I organise fundraising events, bringing people together in the local business community for a day of learning and networking. I commit my expertise and time and, by partnering with others, raise money and awareness.

Promote your sustainability credentials so that customers can see you care about the world beyond your front door. It plays a part in building brand authenticity.

And finally, on our whistle-stop tour of brand building, we reach the final post: continuity.

Continuity

Newly established businesses are curious to know how they can demonstrate continuity. Because if continuity rests on being an established pair of hands, how can you demonstrate continuity as a new business?

You can tick the continuity box by sharing your experience and expertise. If you're starting out with neither – for example, as a new franchisee or licensee – you can lean on the founder's story and the stories of others in the network.

There will be elements of your journey prior to starting your new business, which will help customers see that you are credible and trustworthy. This goes back to sharing your story.

If you're an established business, you can add another layer to your story by demonstrating you're a trusted brand. Underneath the Architectural Plants' name are two words: 'Since 1990'. This tells customers they're a strong, reliable brand; like the mature shrubs, plants and trees grown on site, a business with roots and depth.

Here ends the branding masterclass. Use it to add further lustre and shine to your business brand. Most of my recommendations cost time rather than money. So put your business under the microscope and see what remains for you to build an authentic and magnetic brand.

This is, of course, an ongoing process, one you will enjoy as you see your business unfurl into a remarkable, bold, and brilliant brand.

WOW!! The +1 Model

I love this simple brand-building model. It is based on the simple but often overlooked premise that every communication with a prospect and customer – be it written, phone, email, text, online or face-to-face – is an opportunity to 'WOW' them and so make it more likely they'll choose you, remain loyal to you, and recommend you. It is one of the most powerful tools in your brand-building kit.

How does it work?

You make it your mission to consistently delight your prospects or customers. Delight equals meeting their expectation, plus 1.

+ 1 more contact.

+ 1 moment of real thoughtfulness.

+ 1 extra minute of your time.

+ 1 check to see if all is okay.

The +1 Effect Leads to the WOW Factor

Wow – that's amazing!

Wow – that's what I call service!

Wow – that was thoughtful!

Wow – I didn't expect that!

Wow – I don't believe that!

The Best +1 Factors Meet the Following Criteria

- They're instantly noticed and valued.

- They're quick and easy to implement.

- They cost little or nothing.

- They're implemented on a consistent basis, not just when you're in a good mood or have the time to be thoughtful.

What WOWs are you delivering now?

Does your team have the WOW mindset?

What would it take for you to bring the WOW mindset into every area of your business, from prospecting to delivery, aftercare, resolving customer complaints, and keeping in touch?

Start by talking to your team and making lists of WOWs, adding new ones, and keep the conversation flowing so that great ideas become habits.

Embracing the WOW mindset should be a priority as you strive to build a brand that customers love and keep coming back to, because it is often the smallest touches that have the biggest impact. Be *the* brand that is renowned for putting customers at the centre of their universe.

Your Takeaways

1. Build your personal brand and your business brand together for maximum impact and consistency of communication.

2. Use the Continuum of Behaviour to plan marketing campaigns so messages are accurate, reflecting the relationship with your target audience.

3. What customers think about your business defines and shapes your brand.

4. If you can satisfy customer needs with brilliant service, you have the building blocks of a strong brand.

5. Have you defined the values at the heart of your business, that influence actions and behaviours?

6. Is social media activity separate to your brand-building activities or an integral part?

7. Are you committed to the five pillars of branding?

CHAPTER 4

Being Authentic Is the Ace up Your Sleeve

Step into the spotlight

"... in the brand-building credits bank, your values, integrity, and authenticity count for more than your ability to lead people into a hypnotic trance when you speak..."

A few years ago, a friend attended an event held by a renowned motivational speaker. It was a rock-star production, with music bouncing off the walls, lighting illuminating the speaker, then beaming directly onto audience members, unable to contain their excitement.

According to my friend, the speaker was fierce, loud, and uncompromising. Having seen him online, when he was talking to individuals desperately in need of guidance, he strayed into borderline bullying. There was a lack of emotional intelligence and empathy. It was all about him. It was clear that as his star had ascended, so had his ego. It was now unchecked, fed to the hilt by people spending significant sums to breathe the same air as him.

My friend said that the message he was carrying, with force, was that if he could do it, so could you. If you didn't rise to his elevated status, you'd not tried hard enough. She returned from the conference feeling disillusioned, telling me she could never aspire to be like this man, that she didn't have the enormous character, nor the confidence, to attain a smattering of his success. I wondered why she had attended in the first place. She had been given a free ticket.

If the goal of the conference were to motivate her to stride out, guns blazing, it had failed miserably. When the lights had dimmed, reality began to sink in. I don't dispute this man's style may work for some. They clearly do. He fills rooms with a high ticket price. However, like many people, I don't find this form of motivation motivating. Not in the least.

My friend's dissatisfaction with herself got me thinking about the whole motivational speaker vibe.

Just how significant, and indeed helpful, is a speaker like this man in helping you to build your authentic brand? Please don't think I'm pouring scorn on motivational speakers, per se. Many speakers are genuine, warm, and relatable. They don't want to sell you a system or promise untold wealth. Instead, they want you to tap fully into your talents, find those hidden depths, and remove the barriers stopping you from exploring them and benefiting from them.

Building an authentic brand does not entail being a carbon copy of a person you look up to on the stage, that in real life you wouldn't encounter in a month of Sundays. It's not about filling their shoes or indeed the shoes of any other person, sacrificing elements of your personality and values, in the misguided belief that you're not enough; that the person you're looking up to is the one you should be emulating.

You Are More Than Enough

You do not have to be a polished pro; simply your best authentic self. It is time to be unapologetically you; human and relatable, not robotic, or salesy. Because being original wins trust. Authentic people know what they stand for. They don't need everyone to like them. They place value over validation and are happy to share their story and struggles. They're open about what they've learned, often the hard way, and are still learning.

Crucially, authentic people don't fake it! They recognise that being genuine wins trust and breaks down barriers. They seek to build bridges, not demolish them.

I would imagine you have significant untapped potential. So give yourself time and space to evolve but don't lose sight of your bigger vision, that you want to be authentic and magnetic!

Instead of trying to be like the people that are motivating you to be like them, think like them and sign up to their system, I would encourage you instead to step outside of your comfort zone, and to work on yourself to discover what you're capable of.

This Is Within Your Grasp

Like my friend, when I was new to the world of work, I would find myself at events, feeling like her. Motivated, in awe of the speaker, resolving to mould myself on them, then a few days later feeling disenchanted, back to square one, most of the fist-pumping frenzy forgotten.

In the end, I decided to be happy with myself and focus on being the best version of me, rather than trying to change my character to be like someone else's.

Of course, the closer you are to your authentic self – whether you're speaking to an audience, delivering a workshop, or talking about your latest venture on the radio – the more effortless everything feels. Your confidence grows as you inch into the spotlight.

If you've seen me speaking at an event, you'll know that I wear colourful jackets, jeans, and snazzy trainers. I like sparkly watches and equally sparkly jewellery, and I have a northern accent. I don't use notes or slides, so I occasionally fluff a few lines and I accept this. I feel natural and comfortable, because regardless of where I'm talking, I am authentic. I don't prioritise being polished or sophisticated, wearing designer clothing, or refining my voice. It wouldn't work because it wouldn't be me.

My message – borne out of working with small business owners for 40 years and building my own personal brand – is that you're more than good enough to build your personal brand just as you are. Like most of us, there's room for improvement. This is what you should strive for.

Do you need any superpowers to help you attain the goal of being authentic and magnetic?

Absolutely not!

If you're curious, willing to push forward and challenge yourself, to be honest about what's holding you back, and to embrace the new and unfamiliar, then you're ready to embark on the journey.

Because being authentic should not challenge you.

It starts on territory you're already familiar with, namely understanding your values and living them. As I shared in Chapter 3, your values are the moral compass that guides you, even when times are tough. They reflect how you treat the people around you, regardless of their status, and how you structure your business to be ethical and fair.

Being authentic is about being real, not hiding behind smoke and mirrors, so that every person that connects with you – customers, prospects, networking colleagues, suppliers, and partners – trust you because you're genuine and transparent. They're comfortable in your presence. They keep coming back because you're building relationships that are for the mutual benefit of all. Being authentic means you're not afraid to openly admit to mistakes, share what you've learned, and how you've moved on from them.

I appreciate what business coach Debbie Green has to say about the importance of being your true, authentic self.

"Being yourself really is your biggest advantage. People buy people, right? And, when you stop trying to be what you think others expect and instead show up as who you really are, that's when things start to shift. I've found that the more people tap into their authentic self, through empathy, honesty, curiosity, and courage, the more they connect to the right people, work, and opportunities.

People connect with people, not polish. It's your story, your quirks, your values that make you memorable. I often remind clients: your brand isn't something you create; it's something you reveal. The more grounded you are in your own voice and values, the more magnetic you become. The more self-aware you are and the more you act with intention and awareness of the impact you can (and will) have on people, the more you are being you.

Perfection isn't relatable, but real is. And being real builds trust and respect. Whether you're writing a post, walking into a meeting, or speaking on stage, being authentically you is your ace card. That's what people remember. That's what they're drawn to. That's what people want to see – a person to whom they can relate.

So give yourself permission to stop performing or being fake. Let go of the mask. It drains you of your brilliant energy. Say the thing that feels true. You'll be surprised how powerful it is when your outside world starts to reflect who you really are inside. As I always say, to live a compassionate existence, with effortless presence, empowers you to be the best version of you."

As an authentic person, you don't chase every opportunity, especially those that clash with your integrity and values. And you're comfortable saying no if something does not sit well with you.

Here's what heart-led entrepreneur Debbie Gilbert says about being authentic.

"I've always believed that authenticity is one of the most powerful tools in business. From the very beginning, I've built my businesses around the values of integrity, connection, and genuine support. I'm passionate about helping others succeed, and that means showing up as my true self in every interaction. I don't believe in putting on a front or pretending to be someone I'm not. I'm known for being honest and not sugar-coating my views. What you see is what you get, and I think that's why people trust me and feel comfortable working with me. Over the years, I've found that being authentic builds stronger relationships and it attracts the right opportunities and people. For me, business isn't just about profit; it's about people, purpose, and making a meaningful impact. I'm proud to lead with heart and to inspire others to do the same."

This is what social media expert Michelle Betts told me when I asked her about the importance of being authentic.

"For me, authenticity means showing up as the same person in business that I am in life; kind, honest, and driven by integrity. Authenticity and integrity aren't buzzwords at ByJove Media; they're about backing your values even when no one's watching. Over the years, I've turned down work because it didn't sit right with me. One project conflicted with my ethics, so I walked away. That was hard, but I couldn't compromise my values, even though it meant turning down a paying client. In another case, the client wanted to outsource their social media, but it wasn't what the business really needed. I explained this and supported them in a different way instead. That honesty has never worked against me. If anything, it's helped build long-term trust and relationships I value hugely."

Pause for a moment to reflect on these snippets.

I'm sure you identify wholeheartedly with the traits of an authentic person because you are one. That's great news when it comes to the task of building your personal brand. Because in the brand-building credits bank, your values, integrity, and authenticity count for more than your ability to lead people into a hypnotic trance when you speak, or have them swoon as you enter a room!

Couple this with a willingness to listen to others, to seek feedback from people you trust, and this habit of self-reflection garners you more points when it comes to building your personal brand authentically. Using manipulation techniques from an old sales manual is ineffective by comparison.

Amy Blick has this to say about being authentic.

"Authenticity, to me, means showing up exactly as you are – no inflated promises, no playing small and no trying to be what you think people want you to be. It's the reason my business, exhilHRate, exists. I didn't build a business to 'fit in' with traditional HR. I built one that is bold, commercial, and incorporates value-led behaviours. Staying authentic has meant saying no. No to clients wanting a tick-box HR presence. No to speaking gigs where I'd be expected to fit in with the status quo of transactional HR. And no to work that might have looked shiny on the outside but didn't feel right inside. This has protected my integrity, and it means I attract the right type of client; one that aligns with my values and skill set."

It's inspiring stuff we can all recognise. Being uncompromising, when led by our authenticity, plays a big part in our success.

Finally, here's what bestselling author Stefan Thomas told me about authenticity. I've met Stefan a few times over the years at events where we were keynote speakers. Whilst he undoubtedly has a magnetic presence, the first thing you notice about Stefan is his warmth, followed by his candour.

"I never set out to be authentic. What I mean by that is that I didn't really realise that being authentic was a thing that people aspired to. I did me, and showed up as me, and what I think is interesting is how the reality and authenticity of that has changed over the years. For 20(ish) years, from 1988–2007, I was a full-time estate agent and employed by other people, so my ability to turn up as myself was tempered by other people's expectations of things, such as what I wore, how I styled my hair, and I had to take out the earrings I'd been wearing since 1983! I learnt in that period that authenticity wasn't about what I wore (a formal suit and tie in those days) but more about my values, who I was. I was able to be me, even though I looked quite different to the me you see in 2025. My version of me was based on my core values, of serving others and giving value. Regardless of my career, this stuck with me all the way through.

There are a couple of areas where authenticity and sticking to my values has really helped me. Firstly, I have never been squeamish about selling. If one of my fundamental values is ensuring that people get value, then I know in my heart that what I'm offering them is going to be valuable for them. So I approach anyone I'm selling to, knowing that if they spend £1 with me, they'll get more than £1 back in value. It really helps when I phone potential clients offering them something, because I come from the spirit of genuinely believing it is right for them.

Secondly, sticking to my values helps with any fear of failure. Because my version of success is about being able to show up as me. I can choose the hours I work and these days, what I wear and how I style my hair. The earrings went back in a few years ago."

Is It Time To Step Out of Your Comfort Zone?

If you don't have to be a carbon copy of a fist-pumping, motivational speaker in order to build an authentic and magnetic personal brand, but you're nevertheless aware that, like Kirstie in Chapter 2, there's some way to go on your journey to brand brilliance, what's the next step?

As I mentioned earlier, it's time to step out of your comfort zone and identify what is holding you back; specifically, the barriers to progress that are deep inside and that have nothing to do with what you sell, your sector, or the economy.

Because what's holding you back will thwart your progress in all areas of your business, to a greater or lesser degree. Your brand building – you and your business – will fail to make its mark if you ignore the internal dialogue you're playing without challenging it. The good news is that what you've built for safety over the years can be undone if you're open to change and exploration.

When asked what's holding them back from taking that all-important step to becoming magnetic, most people offer up all manner of excuses. They tend to fall into one of these:

- I'm too busy working to work on myself.

- I feel uncomfortable about being too showy.

- I'm too old to change.

- I don't want to stand out too much.

- The time is not right.

- The hill is too big for me to climb.

- I could never do that.

- I don't do boasting.

And on it goes. However, scratch under the surface of these excuses and you'll find the real reason in one word…

Fear.

Specifically, fear of failure. While other factors may contribute to these excuses, my experience indicates that fear is typically the predominant reason. It keeps us trapped inside our comfort zone until it becomes a straitjacket. The level of fear does not have to be extreme by any stretch of the imagination to halt our progress.

Whether it's a faint rumble or a loud roar, fear must be acknowledged, addressed, and overcome.

Your Takeaways

1. Being relatable and human builds trust. A power persona is exhausting and lacks authenticity.

2. Stepping outside of your comfort zone will help you to flourish.

3. The closer you are to your authentic self, the more comfortable and confident you feel.

4. Curiosity and a willingness to push forward and embrace the new are strong signs you're building an authentic personal brand.

5. Openly admitting some of your mistakes is a strength and to be admired. It makes you relatable.

6. What's holding you back? Is fear undermining your brand building?

CHAPTER 5

Overcoming Fear of Failure

Don't let fear call the shots

"Are you letting opportunities slip under the radar when you should be grabbing them with both hands because you're more than capable?"

A re you wondering why I've included fear of failure in a book about personal branding? Or perhaps you're not surprised, because at times, fear has stopped you from doing something bold and different.

My work has, over many years, given me unrestricted access to many talented and capable businesspeople, often the founders of the businesses themselves. Along the way, I've seen how fear has threatened to hold back some from claiming the spoils of victory.

They feel safe inside their carefully constructed comfort zone. Somewhere along the line, fear of the unknown has been reframed as 'playing it safe'.

The road to successful brand building, where our aim is to be magnetic and dazzling, neither starts nor stays in a comfort zone. If we remain inside it for too long, we become uncomfortable and at odds with our personal ambitions and goals. It's only when we take a bold step outside that we can see the true potential of what lies ahead.

Let me illustrate this with a story that shows how our comfort zone can sabotage us when it is fear-based. I was attending a business event in London. The keynote speaker was a no-show, so the compère filled the time by giving two people on each table a few minutes to talk about their business. He picked me and the man sitting beside me. It was a great opportunity, although I felt a little nervous. As I sat down, the man asked if I would deliver his talk. Thankfully, I was familiar with his sector, so I was able to do his business some justice, even earning a round of applause. He later stated that he was unprepared and concerned about forgetting his points during the presentation. He was a member of a networking group, used to presenting in front of an audience. When I'd been chatting to him beforehand, he appeared confident and assured. In the seconds before his two-minute pitch, fear of failure had taken over. Specifically, fear that he would lose face in front of the people in the room if he did not pull off his talk, so he decided to stay in his comfort zone.

Can you identify with this?

What are you holding back from, because fear is at the root of your unwillingness to do something new or unfamiliar?

How is that fear showing up for you? Procrastination? Finding excuses? Feeling anxious?

Does the thought of trying out new things to promote you and your business lead to feelings of discomfort?

Are you putting barriers in the way of opportunities because fundamentally you don't think you're either capable or good enough?

It's time to be honest because fear is not the friend of being authentic and magnetic. Don't dress fear up as something that's more palatable so that you can dismiss it without further thought. If you feel fearful, you're not alone and it's not insurmountable.

I've experienced fear of failure many times over the years. Its origins can be traced back to my childhood. I eventually realised that if I wanted to claim my power and build my personal brand, then spending time catastrophising and worrying about the 'what ifs' was not going to help me, not one bit.

So what did I do?

I made the decision to change and enrolled in a course of mindful meditation classes, delivered by the Buddhist monks from a nearby temple. I also had several sessions of cognitive behavioural therapy, which enabled me to see fear for what it really was – my mind overthinking, heading down a familiar rabbit hole without reality and the truth interjecting. I absorbed good books, including *Feel the Fear and Do It Anyway* and *The Seven Spiritual Laws of Success*. They reinforced the practical steps I was taking to either eradicate fear from my life or manage it better.

Finally, I began talking about my fears. This was incredibly powerful. When people began to identify with me, I realised I was not alone. I also reduced the concept of fear, from it being a monster that was out to get me, to being something completely natural. I had allowed fear to get out of control, so I visualised putting it back in its box. I accepted that trying out new things in my business was bound to lead to some fear and that was okay. I could manage it. I replaced fearful thoughts with positive ones, focusing on the possible beneficial outcomes of opportunities and visualising them. This has proved to be incredibly effective.

I can occasionally drift into fear, but the difference is that I act despite the fear. And I no longer experience the feeling of impending doom before I'm about to do something that is challenging or new.

I challenge the negative chatterbox with a dominant, kinder voice. If I start thinking about completely losing my thread when I'm public speaking, for example, I tell myself this has never happened and if it does, I'll cope. It's not the end of the world. I'm human, allowed to make mistakes, and the chances are, I'll shine.

Just as you will!

Now, when I'm presented with an opportunity that makes my heart flutter, I say yes because I know the safety net will appear if I find myself falling.

My only regret is not starting this life-affirming work earlier, but for the past 20 years, I've managed fear so much better without it consuming me.

I wanted to bring other people into this chapter, people I respect and that have been successful on their terms. You will recognise them from the previous chapter. I found their candid responses intriguing and uplifting, again reinforcing the fact that when we talk openly about the fears that hold us back, we find ourselves living in the solution.

Debbie Green

"Fear of failure is sneaky!!! It doesn't always shout – it often whispers, 'Maybe I'm not ready. What if I mess this up? Better not risk it.' And before we know it, we've said no to something that could have helped us grow and develop and connect action with our hopes and dreams. I see it all the time – especially when people shy away from making their voice heard in meetings/boardrooms/pitches/media opportunities/networking/public speaking/ or just putting themselves 'out there'.

But here's the thing: fear is part of the process. It doesn't mean stop – it means step forward carefully. You don't need to be fearless to build a bold personal brand, you just need to be a little bit braver than your doubt. You need to listen to your inner-coach rather than your inner-critic and have self-belief in the knowledge that you do know your 'stuff'. If you understand who you are and what you can offer to others, then being able to craft your story to take people on a journey of exploration, empathy, and empowerment – that's your superpower.

I always encourage people to shift the focus. Instead of asking, 'What if I fail?' I ask, 'What if I don't?' When you show up – even if your voice shakes – you build resilience and confidence over time. It's not about being perfect and polished. It's about being present and being you – a person who can connect with others on a human level. And you know you can do that.

Often, the very thing you're scared of doing is the thing that will elevate your brand, your confidence, and your impact. So take the opportunity grab that mic, say yes, tell your story. You never know who's waiting to hear it and who you'll inspire just by being you."

Debbie Gilbert

"As the eldest child, I was often the one doing things first, which helped reduce my fear of failure from a young age. I was always described as confident and outgoing. While I've never been fearless (heights and spiders still make me squirm!), I've learned to overcome many anxieties, like my former fear of needles!

When I started my business in 1998, fear didn't hold me back. It wasn't a bold leap. It was a necessity, driven by personal circumstances at the time. As the business grew, I saw an opportunity to build a community through networking events. To begin with, I invested in a franchise; buying into an existing brand felt like a safer route to help mitigate risk.

I'll admit I was more daunted than afraid. I still remember the first event I ever hosted. I felt physically sick, and my legs were shaking as I took to the floor. But I did it. Just 18 months in, the franchisor went into liquidation. By then, I had built four successful groups with 150 members, so I took the leap and created my own networking company. Over time, it expanded, and I brought in group leaders to help run more events, which are still running today.

The phrase 'feel the fear and do it anyway' has always stuck with me. My philosophy has always been 'better done than perfect'. If something doesn't go as planned, you learn from it, and I never use the word 'fail'.

In 2015, I launched The Best Businesswomen Awards. At the time, some people thought it might not succeed. Setting up a UK-based awards programme was a big risk, especially when awards weren't as mainstream as they are now.

But I approached it the same way I approach everything in business by asking myself, 'What's the worst that can happen? Is it worth the time and effort?'

Looking back, I'm proud of how much I've achieved, not because I had no fear but because I refused to let fear stop me. In business, it's about assessing risks and mitigating them. To be successful in business, you must learn to push fears to one side and be open to learning and adapting your plans. Gaining expert advice and support and accepting that you don't know everything is vital."

Michelle Betts

"I've experienced fear of failure, especially imposter syndrome! I'm lucky to have a brilliant support network and mentors who help me keep it in check. I also keep it at bay by staying up to date through training and conferences, because I always want to have the latest information at my fingertips.

When I wrote my first novel, *Smoke and Mirrors*, the imposter syndrome came back hard. I shared it with a few trusted, critical friends and braced myself for the worst. Their feedback gave me the confidence to keep going.

My best advice? Ask for support. Don't isolate yourself. Say yes, then work out how. That's how I've built my business and kept moving forward on my terms, and without losing who I am along the way."

Amy Blick

"I had a fear of failure when I launched my business, ExhilHRate. I had to get used to the difference between a monthly salary, versus billing for my output and delivery. I still had the nervous little butterflies until a year ago. Nowadays I am doing myself a complete disservice if I show up as an overthinking people-pleaser. I have learned to reframe the feeling of nervousness into excitement.

I ask myself, 'What's the worst that could happen?' I plan for that and proceed regardless! I also surround myself with people that love working outside of their comfort zone and making money. Success on your own terms? That's the good stuff!"

Wisdom From One of the Top 101 Global Influencers, David Beeney

Author of the bestselling book *Breaking the Silence*, David's mission is to make the whole arena of mental health free of stigma and judgement, so that more people can share and seek help without fear of reprisal. He's a key person of influence on the global stage, with his wisdom, experience, and expertise sought by household brands and SMEs worldwide. David's book cover image was taken by photographer Rankin. David uses this startling admission as an icebreaker at his workshops, seminars, and book signings.

In his words…

Turning Your Fear of Failure Into Your Superpower

"Even though I became the managing director of a daily newspaper by the age of 35, I fell a long way from fulfilling my true potential. I was lucky to have been gifted with strong leadership skills and had been predicted from a young age to reach dizzy heights! However, in my forties, I completely lost my way and even spent a ridiculous eight years at the risk of redundancy, watching many people with less talent go sailing past me. By the time I reached 50, I had completely lost my self-worth, and my career was dead and buried.

Looking back, why did my career fall apart when it was all set to flourish? Simple... I feared having a panic attack in front of my colleagues and having my mental health exposed. In short, I had a huge fear of failure.

My life completely turned around just before my 54th birthday when I chose to 'out myself' about my mental health. Later that year, I founded Breaking the Silence and within two years was recognised as being one of the top 101 global influencers on employee engagement.

In the last nine years, I have delivered over 1,000 talks to more than 50,000 people and have also become an author. My client list includes Google, The Royal Navy, McDonald's, Sainsbury's, HSBC, Mercedes F1 and the United Nations.

So what has enabled my success?

How have I gone from years of avoiding public speaking, to being one of most renowned keynote speakers on mental health in the UK?

Answer: I have given myself permission to fail.

Looking back, I spent too many years fighting my anxiety when I should have made it my best friend. I spent too much time trying to be perfect and being far too hard on myself.

For those people who live in fear of failure, I hope you discover much earlier in life than me that people get inspired by vulnerability and it is 'okay not to be okay.' Be kinder to yourself and accept not everything will go to plan.

When you take the pressure off yourself to be perfect, you will feel more relaxed and have greater clarity of thought. We all know this is when we can optimise our creativity and productivity.

I have just turned 63 years old, and I am enjoying the best time of my life, all because my 'fear of failure' has become my superpower!"

I hope you feel inspired by these people, and you can identify with much of what has been shared. Recognise fear for the imposter it is, start talking about it openly, and take strides to reducing it or removing it altogether. You're not alone, and you are doing something about it which is an act of courage. As you begin to ease fear out of your life, you will feel more powerful, more confident, and much more open to opportunities.

I wanted to share this article that I wrote for my monthly column, 'Living Well with Dee,' in *Health Triangle Magazine*. This hit the right note with readers and is the perfect way to end a chapter on overcoming fear of failure. Especially the last sentence. I hope you agree.

Face Your Fears. And Flourish.

When a client casually commented I should write a book, my first thoughts were to dismiss it outright. What authority did I have to write a book? How would I cope with negative reviews? What if my book sank into obscurity? Once I'd let the negative chatterbox run its course, I pondered his suggestion, allowing myself to daydream. Writing a book had been in my mind since the tender age of eight.

Thankfully, I let a positive voice prevail and what was one tentative book became five, with my most recent book, *The Boutique*, published a few months ago. My journey as an author has been enthralling and amazing with two publishing contracts, several awards, and thousands of lovely readers all over the world. Three of my books have become number one bestsellers. Of course, like most authors, I've had my share of one-star reviews in amongst the hundreds of five stars, coupled with episodes of imposter syndrome. I coped!

Let me explain why my initial reaction was to say no. You may identify with my skewed thinking.

I rejected the suggestion because I was fearful of the unknown, of putting myself 'out there,' of being criticised; fundamentally of being a failure. It was a pattern that was so familiar, a comfort blanket that was fast becoming oppressive and uncomfortable. It was much easier to swat the idea and not put myself in the firing line of failure, than it was to explore something new and exciting with a curious, enlivened mind. In that moment, I could see how fear of failure was suffocating me. It had driven me on at school but at a price; my anxiety skyrocketing because I never felt good enough. As a young girl, I remember repeating the mantra that I could not fail instead of feeling excited at the prospect of success.

That day with my client, I had something of an epiphany. I decided to act despite the fear. I told myself I was more than capable of managing what would surely come my way as a published author – the good and the not so good!

Today, whilst I still experience fear – when public speaking, for example, or tackling an unfamiliar task that is not my strong suit – I don't let it stop me. I remind myself that I'm good enough and, hey, if I fall at the first hurdle, it wasn't for me anyway. Or I can ask for help and try again. *Feel the Fear and Do it Anyway* has been my go-to book. I highly recommend it if you're stuck in a cycle of fear.

What are you letting pass you by because you're afraid of failure? Is your decision-making underpinned by irrational fears? Are you letting opportunities slip under the radar, when in fact you should be grabbing them with both hands because you're more than capable?

I don't like to think of where I would be today, had I allowed fear to continue ruling my life, my dream of becoming a successful author fading fast. Writing books really has been the making of me, opening many doors with a myriad of exciting opportunities behind them. I've connected with incredible people, had one of my books translated into Chinese, and written a short story book – another cherished ambition.

Is a little soul searching overdue for you? It's neither life affirming nor healthy to let fear inhabit our minds unchallenged. Our time on this planet is precious. We must make the most of it.

Don't let fear call the shots.

Your Takeaways

1. Many of us feel happy inside our comfort zone until it starts to feel like a straitjacket. Is that you?

2. When you break free of limiting beliefs and behaviours, you can see the full potential of what lies ahead.

3. If fear is undermining you, take empowering and practical steps to reduce its impact and eliminate it altogether.

4. Give yourself permission to fail and permission to succeed.

5. Sometimes, you must acknowledge fear and act despite it.

CHAPTER 6

Finding Your Whys

The rocket fuel that helps you focus

"Sometimes, the big wins drop into your lap early on; other times you're several months down the line, wondering if the miracle will ever happen, and kapow – you've hit the jackpot."

In this chapter, we look at the reasons why you want to build an authentic and magnetic personal brand, because they pave the way for your personal brand plan.

The reasons behind your willingness to invest your time and energy in a cause of significance – personal, business, or both – must be compelling if you're to see it through. Sometimes, the big brand wins drop into your lap early on; sometimes, you're several months down the line, wondering if the miracle will ever happen, and kapow – you've hit the jackpot.

Brand building does not happen overnight. However, if you apply the tips and strategies in this book as you start or restart your personal branding adventure, it will bear fruit faster than you thought. Your commitment is the time you will dedicate, over and above the time you currently spend on your business.

Your 'Why' will keep you going on days when it's a challenge to muster any enthusiasm; you may have a setback that affects your confidence, and you find yourself doubting your ability to get anything right. We've all been there. It's a rite of passage for the tenacious and talented business owner.

Your 'Why' will keep you connected to the brand-building cause, even when you're unable to do much more than make it to the end of the day intact. It may be that after a period of business pressure, you need time to dust yourself down and take a dose of positive self-talk before stepping into the shoes of building your personal brand again.

How do you embark on your personal brand building journey?

By understanding that your 'Whys' are your rocket fuel.

Here are 21. Which ones do you identify with the most?

Many are connected. For example: you may want to be seen as an authentic, approachable, and generous person in your sector (1) and an exemplar in your sector (2), because this will shorten the time it takes for a client to do business with you (3), and it will lead to more business (4) and (6). You may want to raise funds for your charities (15) and attract talented people (16), so it's important to be perceived as authentic, approachable, and generous (1).

The more reasons you tick, the better, especially when you can see the connections forming. Expand on each reason with your thoughts, as you can incorporate these into your personal brand plan.

1. My objective is to be recognised within my sector as an authentic, approachable, and generous individual.

2. I want to be recognised as an exemplar in my sector, leading with my knowledge, experience, and integrity.

3. I want to shorten the length of time it takes for a customer to know, like, and trust me.

4. I want to increase my pool of potential customers.

5. I want to become the *sought after*, not the *seeker* of business, so my role leans into evaluating opportunities, not constantly hunting for customers.

6. I want to take my business to the next level.

7. I want to write a book that is well received and recognised by my peers/my professional body/my membership association.

8. I want to become an accomplished public speaker.

9. I want to increase my fees to reflect my expertise.

10. I want to be open to opportunities for self-development.

11. I want to be a trusted voice for the media, so I am sought for comment and articles.

12. I want to protect my business from the impact of tough times.

13. I want it to be easier for me to enter new markets.

14. I want to enjoy the recognition that comes from an amazing reputation.

15. I want to support charities and open more doors for them, raising funds by using my name and reputation.

16. I want to attract more high calibre people to collaborate with me on the initiatives I'm planning.

17. I want to undertake continuous professional development to build on my experience and gain new qualifications.

18. I want to show the people I care for and respect that I have what it takes to build an authentic and magnetic brand.

19. I want to hold sell-out seminars, conferences, and masterclasses.

20. I want to build an income stream from writing online.

21. I want to be the absolute best person in business that I can be, so this process is an integral part of my journey.

As you work through this list, ticking the reasons that resonate, allocate a score for each one, with five being the maximum, one the lowest. If you allocate five, it is particularly important to you. Add any other reasons not on the list and score them appropriately.

Your list of compelling reasons function as a compass, guiding you, reminding you why you're committing energy and time to building your personal brand. Don't be afraid to add new reasons and to change your scores. When you start working on your personal brand plan in the next chapter, include your list with the additional information you've written.

Be prepared for some of your 'Whys' to assume a greater importance than initially anticipated. When I undertook this exercise several years ago, my strongest personal brand building reasons were: 1, 2, 3, 4, 5, 7, 8, 10 and 11. They were connected, and each was given a rating of five. It made sense, because at the same time as building my business, I also wanted to write a bestselling book. I knew that having a great reputation as a marketer would increase book sales and open doors. At the same time as writing books, I had to keep the focus on my business on earning fees. My husband had given up a well-paid job to support me. Having a stellar reputation as a person of influence would land me more clients. It would also shorten the time between a person enquiring about my services, to becoming a paid client.

When I was writing books, my focus was on hitting the bestsellers, but only by creating content that readers would find invaluable. I didn't want my efforts to vanish into the graveyard of unwanted books! My books had to generate their own income streams.

These were all robust reasons for me to build my personal brand, even when sometimes I wanted to be invisible; usually after reading a one-star review.

However, in recent years, the need to earn money has diminished, and my focus has shifted to using my personal brand to raise awareness of charities close to my heart and to find ways of financially supporting them. I also want to attract like-minded people to collaborate with me on exciting projects that support local businesses and raise money for charity. With this book, I have once again dipped my toes into pitching for public speaking engagements and writing for magazines that are read by my target audiences. A launch conference based on *You're the Best!* is planned, giving me even more reasons to get involved. My reasons now for strengthening my personal brand are 7, 10, 14, 15, 16, 19 and 21.

This simple exercise helps clarify what you genuinely want from your personal brand.

Building your business and personal brand should be an enjoyable, life-affirming process, not least because there will be times when incredible opportunities fall into your lap.

This is not good luck.

It's your reward for being on high alert to opportunities. Others may be waiting for things to happen but you're out there, making them happen. Because of this, you'll reach a tipping point.

The tide is turning in your favour.

Instead of always reaching out to others, people are approaching you because they have heard great things about you, read your content, seen you speak, heard your podcast, and more. These people are likely to be potential customers, influencers, journalists, event organisers, and membership organisations.

You'll also find that when you do nudge a door – for example, you're interested in writing a column for a magazine – the editor has already heard about you, so the reaction is positive and you don't have to pitch.

Again, this is not luck.

It's a culmination of the energy you're bringing to every interaction, to every person, everywhere you go.

You're becoming magnetic, without even being aware of it.

You've aligned your expertise, your 'Whys' and commitment to building your brand, to create a powerful pull. If people don't include you, they're the ones missing out.

Let me illustrate these points in action.

I pitched an interview about my short story book, *The Boutique*, to a local magazine editor. He replied within a few days, agreeing to the interview. He'd been reading my top tips blogs for authors and was interested in finding out more. My interview is now in 100,000 printed magazines. I also suggested a business column, using some of the material in *You're the Best!* I was met with another yes.

In the last week, I've been approached by a writers' group to run a writing workshop, followed by a book signing. The organiser had seen my Facebook posts, promoting my book signing at Waterstones bookshop. I could go on because every week there is something new for me to consider. It may be a speaking engagement, a book signing, an article, or a radio interview. When I approached the people who contributed to this book, I was thrilled by the positive reaction from every person.

Make sure to be on high alert for opportunities when you're out and about. I'm always in this mode. For example, I recently visited a client at an event in Birmingham. I took advantage of a quiet spell to call in on three magazine editors that were exhibiting at the show. I chatted to each one about this book and how every businessperson should focus on building their personal brand. All three confirmed they would like to serialise *You're the Best!* including an interview with me.

Fortune favours the generous, the brave, and the trophy hunters, so don't hold back and don't be afraid to seize the moment!

I hope you can see how the process of building your personal brand will lead to great things. You set the train of events in motion, with your energy, your focus, and your authenticity. The magnetic part of your personal brand building is slowly unfurling at this stage. So create your list and apply your scores. Review it to ensure you're happy with what you see; that it conveys the reasons why you want to build an authentic and magnetic personal brand.

Then keep it close to hand for your personal brand plan, which is the next step. You're about to go further on this exciting and creative journey.

Your Takeaways

1. Connect with your 'Whys' and you will see things through, even when you're being pulled in all directions.

2. Time over money is the precious commodity required to build your personal brand.

3. When times are challenging, you can lay down your personal brand building tools, but don't leave it too long before picking them up.

4. Score your 'Whys', spend time thinking about them, and don't be afraid to add new ones. They connect you to your brand building.

5. Look for the natural synergy between your 'Whys'.

6. The positive energy you bring to every interaction means that people will start looking for you. Doors will open magically.

CHAPTER 7

Developing Your Personal Brand Plan

It's business and it's personal

"I want to encourage you to take that important step into the spotlight so you can claim your rightful space as an authentic and magnetic personal brand!"

Conducting a marketing audit is usually the first task when a new client brings me into their business. It uncovers the areas where improvements are long overdue. Two of the biggest areas marked 'significant room for improvement'? The perception of marketing as 'nice to have, but not necessary' and the lack of resources the business allocates to marketing – human and financial.

When the fires have been extinguished and we've established marketing in its rightful place as the engine that drives the business, we turn our attention to the marketing strategy; the essential task before we embark on the tactics. This encompasses many things including:

1.   The target audiences, from existing customers to cold prospects, influencers, and introducers.

2.   The reasons why my client wants to target each group.

3. Understanding the objections to my client's products or services from the different audiences.

4. Identifying the needs of each audience for my client's offering.

5. Developing the compelling sales messages for each audience, anchored in relevant market trends, buying behaviours and benefits.

6. Determining how we locate each audience so we can target them.

7. Establishing in principle the promotional plans.

I'm sharing this because your personal brand plan should ideally run parallel to your marketing strategy. You're not redoubling your effort and time because there will be significant areas of overlap. Whether you're promoting yourself or your business, your target audiences will be the same as will their needs, the messages you use to draw them in, and how you locate them. You're marshalling all the valuable resources (this includes you!) at your disposal to promote your business. This is time well spent, not least because it puts an end to shoot-from-the-hip marketing activities.

You don't have to be an experienced marketing pro to get results. Making sure you're organised, that time is allocated to marketing, and you have the necessary support to craft content and begin targeting your audiences does not require marketing skills. It's as much about setting time aside for marketing and putting the plan into action as it is about being creative.

When I explain this to a business owner keen to promote their business and become a person of influence, their relief is palpable. They can see that with some long-overdue changes, they can chip away at the marketing coal face and start to get results.

Is This Your Time?

Many businesspeople warm to the idea of building an authentic personal brand and becoming leading influencers in their field, alongside the task of growing their business. Reasons vary. But, at some stage, they've recognised that their skills, experience, and expertise are moving them into that space. Or they've seen others, with lesser credentials, claiming the spotlight and reaping the rewards.

It's their time. I hope it's yours.

In this chapter, I share the roadmap I created when I decided to elevate my profile, become a person of influence, and reap the rewards as a published author. I hope to encourage you to take that critical step into the spotlight, so you can claim your rightful space as an authentic and magnetic personal brand.

Because you were not destined to live life in the shadows.

You deserve to leverage your expertise and experience. And this entails stepping out and stepping up! Look upon this activity as the exciting part of your journey to be enjoyed, not feared. Embrace it with an abundant mindset that you're worthy of the recognition that will surely follow, and that you have much value to share.

You've no doubt made progress already with your list of 'Whys'. It's time to become more visible, recognised, and rewarded.

Your Expertise as a Person of Influence Can Be Narrow or Broad

A genuine expert resides in many of us. For some, expertise can be niche; for others it may be broader. We know an awful lot about an awful lot!

Reassuringly, expertise is not dependent on attaining academic qualifications. Some people are indeed renowned for their commitment to study, but many more are respected for their knowledge and expertise, born of experience. If a demand exists for yours, no matter how narrow or broad, it's enough to begin the journey.

What Defines a Person of Influence?

A person of influence is someone we look to for trusted and helpful advice. They're not defined by money or wealth. They have a deep-seated desire to share their knowledge and expertise, so others can benefit. And this is the case, whether money has changed hands or not. They're magnetic people, nurturing a strong desire to help. They create with purpose and passion, and are generous, curious, and enthusiastic.

They're not content to settle for the know-how and skills they've already accrued. They want to learn more and to share this with their tribes. People of influence are often found at the forefront of their field, familiar with new ideas, upcoming products, the latest trends, and research in their sector.

They continue searching when others have stopped.

In business circles, they have an enviable record. They do not hoard their knowledge and tend to give freely before expecting clients, money, or likes.

They command attention because they have gravitas.

They speak at seminars, exhibitions, and conferences. Editors, journalists, and bloggers value their opinions. They're invited to write articles, speak on podcasts, create sponsored content, run webinars, and present at major events. Their peers and target audiences see them as trusted, reliable sources of relevant information and expertise. They're magnetic because they create with purpose.

Do you recognise a little, or indeed a lot, of yourself in this description? It may be that although you have much of value to share, you've not yet embarked on the public facing part of your journey.

The Benefits of Being Magnetic and a Key Person of Influence

They're not dissimilar to those of a strong business brand.

- Unlike competitors that struggle when times are tough, a person of influence does not feel the pinch. And in good times, they're turning work away or recruiting. Their reputation, combined with being in demand, is rocket fuel for business success.

- They repurpose their knowledge and expertise to create new products, services, and income streams, often from just one idea or eureka moment, which they bring to life.

- They're often given first refusal to work on profitable and exciting business opportunities. And they enjoy collaborating with other people that are leaders in their respective sectors.

- They attract a greater share of business than their competitors, without having to fight for it. Others are drawn to them because of their status.

When you start to reap the rewards of your influencer status, your personal brand has entered the realm of attraction over promotion.

Are You Reluctant To See Yourself as a Person of Influence?

Something that holds us back from seeing ourselves in this light is the fear that others know more. As I mentioned in Chapter 1, this dominated my thoughts when writing my first book. I spent too much time thinking about other marketers, who I was convinced knew far more than I did. Looking back, it seems such a waste of energy! I urge you to set aside those limiting beliefs that bring nothing of value to your life.

Focus instead on the knowledge and experience you're more than capable of sharing. There's room in any sector, any business community, for many great people to command attention and respect.

And that includes you!

I've also seen the tendency of talented people to downplay their knowledge as common sense. Are you guilty of this? I was; I still am at times.

Your common sense is the result of many years of dedication and hard work. It's anything but common to those keen to learn from you and be associated with you.

It was only when I was in the company of other marketers, at events organised by The Chartered Institute of Marketing, that I grasped the extent of my knowledge and experience.

You may also be concerned that within your sector are several established, influential people. How can you enter and claim your spot?

You can and you should!

In the small business community, for example, you'll find many influencers working in the same field, each one holding a position of respect and authority with their following of fans and advocates.

There's always room for an authentic and magnetic person of influence to enter an established space and find theirs.

Do You Need a Significant Social Following To Be a Person of Influence?

It's tempting to think you need thousands of followers to achieve influencer status, especially when many influencers in the consumer field, such as celebrities, sell masses of products with a few video posts.

Reassuringly, you don't need this level of status. People of influence tend to find their own niche of people that want to align with them. This can include interest groups, readers of publications, membership associations, and their existing networks. They grow their tribes on the simple premise of advocacy – one loyal follower recommending them to another. People of influence are not swayed by the number of likes or the social algorithms. They focus on making a positive impact through consistent, relevant contributions, rather than obsessing over likes. They're intent on building community and trust, placing value on conversations, and sharing material relevant to their following.

A big social following undoubtedly amplifies their voice, but their niche network is more important to them than a huge social following, as it's more geared towards simply liking their posts when they glance at them in their feed, rather than venturing much further. Add the task of cultivating your online following to your personal brand plan if you're confident this will give you the reach you're looking for, but not at the detriment of focusing on the specific groups that you can access with relative ease and where you know you're likely to have the greatest impact.

Building Your Influencer Status

The steps that follow will help you create a workable personal brand plan. Capture your thoughts as you work through each section.

1. **Why do you want to be considered a person of influence?**

    You're likely to have many reasons ranging from commercial to altruism.

    *   To create new business opportunities.

    *   To differentiate from competitors.

    *   To do some good by sharing your experience and expertise freely, including with those that cannot afford to work with you.

    *   To advance the professional standards in your sector.

    *   To make a sale easier by shortening the decision-making process.

    *   To help retain customers.

    *   To acquire new, bigger, and more profitable customers than your current customer base.

    *   To increase the likelihood of new products or services being successful.

- To build a local, national, and international reputation.

- To charge more.

- To help recession-proof your business.

- To make you feel good about yourself – self-fulfilment!

Revisit Chapter 6 to bring your 'Whys' into this part of your plan.

2. **What are you bringing to the table to establish yourself as a credible person of influence?**

It's time to undertake a personal stock take. What have you achieved to date in your career and even prior to this? Use the following to guide you:

- A summary of your expertise.

- A summary of your experience.

- A list of your skills.

- A summary of the standout results and positive outcomes you've achieved for customers and other target audiences.

- A list of your qualifications, training, membership of prestigious bodies, and accreditations.

- Details of your programme of continuous professional development.

- Any awards you have won.

- Any achievements that elicit a "Wow!".

- A summary of your commitment to sustainability.

When you look at your answers, I hope you're pleasantly surprised and that any residual doubts are now easing out.

3. Are there any gaps?

Having audited your skills and experience, you should be impressed. Are there gaps to address? I realised I had to improve my knowledge of strategic marketing planning. A potential client had even commented on this, so I wanted to address it – and fast! A short online training course and a study book from The Chartered Institute of Marketing filled the gap. How can you plug your gap without taking too much time? Your gaps may be in personal development. Filling them does not have to be onerous.

For example:

- Could you consider joining a professional body aligned with your profession? Andy Moylan, a former client, is an experienced trade credit insurance broker. He joined The Chartered Institute of Credit Management (CICM) to share his knowledge and learn new insights. When he enquired about joining, he was awarded the Fellowship status within a few weeks. This unexpected and prestigious recognition helped boost his status as a person of influence. I was surprised to discover that as part of my Fellowship benefits package, I qualify for free online learning. Subjects range from presentation skills to social media training.

- Are there seminars, training events, or conferences you could attend to enhance your soft skills and learning? With bite-sized online training, it's easy to plug learning into our lives.

- Can you join discussion groups with your peers on social platforms such as LinkedIn and on websites that serve your sector? Should you be contributing to forums organised by your professional body or membership association? Andy began speaking at webinars organised by the CICM. He also joined professional forums to share his expertise. Once his name had become renowned in professional circles, it was only a matter of months before he was invited to speak at a major export conference. He was also signed up as a contributor to *The Exporter Magazine*. Andy has since spoken at many global events and presented several high-profile webinars.

- Are there books that you would you benefit from reading, plus white papers, blogs, and magazines you could subscribe to?

- Do opportunities exist for you to gain new qualifications or accreditations?

- Could you commit to a programme of continuous professional development through a relevant professional body, so ongoing learning runs in parallel to your personal brand building? This may also lead to additional qualifications.

Ongoing learning is important, not least because it keeps your personal brand evolving. But don't make it onerous. You have a business to run so start with the things that are easy to accomplish.

4. Who needs to know about you?

You want to be on the radar of your target audiences; the people that can buy from you, learn from you, recommend you, and advocate for you. It's advisable to avoid targeting everyone; you'll run out of steam and patience! Consider instead the people and groups you want to build a relationship with and that are worthy of your time. These are the target audiences I ask clients to identify in their marketing strategy.

For example:

- Your customers. Enhancing their perception of you will further strengthen their loyalty and provide more reasons for them to recommend you.

- Charities. Are there charities and volunteer groups you'd like to work with on a no-fee basis as part of your commitment to sustainability?

- New businesses. Could you offer your expertise freely as a mentor to a few new businesses in your sector?

- Your lapsed customers. Making them aware of everything you have to offer and your growing reputation could revive some relationships.

- Cold prospects. These are the specific groups that have a need to buy what you offer, and you have prioritised them for targeting.

- Introducers, influencers, and referrers. These are the people and groups that could lead to new customers and to opportunities that will help you to build your personal brand and business brand. Again, you will have identified these if you have worked on your marketing strategy.

- Strategic partners. These can include your peers, hand selected by you for joint ventures.

- Specific editors and journalists. This is relevant when you're targeting publications, including the ones read by your peers and target audiences. Editors are always looking for interesting personal stories and expert columns.

- Your suppliers. Making them aware of your enhanced status could lead to better payment terms and preferential treatment when supplies are limited or indeed plentiful.

5. **Promoting your influencer status through several platforms.**

    To be influential, share your content across various platforms. Consider the following:

    - The online and printed papers, journals, and magazines to which you could contribute.

    - Blogging. Could you share your wisdom in your own dedicated blog and vlog? Could you respond to content on sites and forums popular with your audiences? Could you write guest posts and share top tips video content?

    - Podcasts and webinars. Can you create your own and be a contributor on others?

    - Radio. There are now many popular independent shows, encompassing a broad spectrum of business and wellbeing themes. Could you be interviewed, or even present a show?

    - Social media. Should you review your social media strategy and make a conscious effort to share tips and useful information regularly with your followers? Could you comment on the posts of complementary influencers? Do you need to respond more fully to the people that comment on your posts?

    - Public speaking. Are there opportunities for you to speak at conferences and events that your target audiences will attend? Are there local exhibitions or networking groups at which you could speak?

- Hosting your own events. Could you organise online seminars, in-person conferences, and masterclasses?

Dig into the detail with your answers. This is not the time for impressive statements that cannot be qualified. You will have to go away, do your research, and then come back to expand on a point and convert it into an action. As I mentioned in Chapter 6, you'll see a pattern emerging where planned activities combine to create one big, positive impression.

For example, I was recently interviewed by Janine Lowe on UK Health Radio, the world's biggest health radio station. Janine had messaged me on Facebook, saying: "I'm seeing you everywhere, Dee, and reading about you. I would love to interview you for my show." Had I been sitting in a room, crossing my fingers that my latest book would gain traction of its own accord, I would've been waiting a long time. You must be the architect of your own success, but as discussed earlier, you will reach that tipping point if you stick at it.

6. **Do your marketing communications convey your key person status?**

Perform a stock take of your marketing collateral, online and print, to ensure that your status as a person of influence shines through. Update it as your star continues to rise.

For example:

- Your website. Does this include information about your knowledge, skills, experience, training, and qualifications, making it abundantly clear you're the go-to person in your sector? Could you add the logos from the membership associations and professional bodies you belong to? Would a Press page on your website inform journalists of your availability for comments? Should you update client testimonials and add new client case studies? Could you add short videos sharing your business story, what you offer, and any insights on trends that would capture visitor interest?

- Your literature online and print. Are you displaying your key person of influence status for people to discover more about you? Is your focus solely on describing what you offer? Is there an opportunity to provide prospects and customers with a précis of your experience and how, as a person of influence, you add value to any relationship?

- Your social media profiles. Are they so informal that when a person is doing their homework on you, they form an impression that falls short of what you're hoping for? Are they incomplete, in need of a radical overhaul, or require some tweaking?

7. **Can you build new income streams?**

You may find that your influencer status paves the way for new income-generating initiatives.

For example, could you...

- Run delegate-based seminars, conferences, exhibitions, or masterclasses?

- Create bite-sized online training?

- Develop a membership club?

- Charge for some of your online material?

- Amalgamate existing content you've created into white papers, study guides, or technical sheets?

- Charge for some of the events you speak at?

- Develop mentoring/coaching programmes?

- Write a book?

Some of these may appeal now because they're straightforward to implement; others can go on the back burner for when you have more confidence, contacts, and time!

Like anything worth pursuing, becoming a magnetic person of influence requires dedication, consistency, passion, and a plan.

If you love what you do and are already on the road to building an authentic and magnetic brand, use your plan to provide a springboard for the next steps. Your plan underscores your motivation for becoming a person of influence, outlines your strengths, and describes how you'll take on a more visible, initiative-taking role.

You will enjoy the process and the recognition that comes with it. And not simply because of a healthier bank balance. Ask most influencers what they love, and they'll tell you that helping others and seeing the impact of their contributions are the best rewards of all.

Special Focus: Lumpy Mail – Brand Building Just Got a Whole Lot More Personal!

For decades, I've been a fan of small business owners using lumpy mail to draw attention to their brand – business and personal. For example, a coaster made from recycled materials in your brand colours, a quality pen with the initials of the person you're targeting, or a snazzy mug will stop the recipient in their tracks and enliven their mind to receive your accompanying message. Many years ago, I targeted three elusive business founders with a personal letter and a fountain pen bearing their initials. My client had found it impossible to get past the gatekeeper and secure a meeting. The pens were effective in all three cases. She got her meetings and signed up two new clients.

Today, I received a handwritten envelope through the post, which certainly caught my interest, especially the 'Do Not Bend' message that intrigued me. Inside were two cards, each one an original watercolour. They were exquisite cameos of wild flowers. One of the cards bore a message from

Angus Grady, a renowned marketing professional who has built his name with thousands of business owners on 'starting conversations that convert'.

It read: 'Dee, what a joy to see your name on my post and thank you for the lovely comments. My new door opener, hand painted cards. Chat soon, I hope. Angus X'

There was also a QR code with the message, 'This is a friendly link, just a quick message for you'.

The other card was blank, accompanied by a matching envelope, clearly intended for my use.

To say I was impressed by such a thoughtful and personal gesture is an understatement. It stopped me in my tracks, and I messaged my publisher saying we had to include this section in my book.

As an example of how to build an authentic and magnetic personal brand, this ticked every single box. Of course, it helps that Angus is an accomplished painter, but this should not stop you from thinking about how you can build your personal brand in attention-grabbing ways. You may have several VIPs you want to reach, including editors, journalists, potential clients, and influencers. They warrant something more than just a standard email, even a standalone letter. Sending a letter through the post with a high-quality 'lumpy' element could tip the scales in your favour. It's something I've done for years, with the lumpy enclosures ranging from quality teabags to coasters, handmade organic chocolates, and bookmarks. These inexpensive inclusions have enabled me to start meaningful conversations with elusive people, protected by zealous assistants and gatekeepers. And like Angus, they help in building my personal brand.

As part of your personal brand plan, consider incorporating lumpy mail as a proven strategy for VIPs. Make sure that the person you're targeting will respond favourably. A cheap enclosure will not cut it so make it relevant, charming and meaningful, with the goal that it should lead to a conversation in every case, because your personal brand is built on conversations that convert.

Your Takeaways

1. Your personal brand plan is like your marketing strategy, so expect several areas of overlap.

2. Being organised, clear on your objectives, and devoting time to creating your personal brand plan does not require marketing expertise.

3. You were not destined to live life in the shadows. You were born to shine.

4. People of influence are magnetic because they create with purpose and passion.

5. When your influencer status starts being recognised, you've entered the realm of attraction over promotion.

6. Don't downgrade your hard-won expertise and experience as common sense.

7. A commitment to ongoing learning keeps your personal brand evolving.

CHAPTER 8

How to Build a Magnetic Personal Brand

Into action!

"One of the benefits of connection is that you start to see results early on. When people see you 'popping' up everywhere, their curiosity turns to a fear of missing out."

In the previous chapters, I've focused on how you can build a compelling and authentic personal brand. As you work through this process, you will undoubtedly experience moments, and occasions, when you can see the magnetic part of your personal brand rising to the fore. People are now starting to look for you.

This is natural, exciting, and flattering. You've earned it.

With the momentum you're building with your target audiences and the eureka moments – a consequence of your personal brand plan – it's inevitable that you will start to move from being the *seeker* of work and opportunities, to being the *sought after*.

You can accelerate the pace of progress if you make a concerted effort to build on the magnetic part of your personal brand, rather than waiting for it to happen organically.

Now is the time to put your personal brand plan into action!

By working through your plan, you'll eventually find yourself with so many offers and opportunities that you can take your time deliberating over them, cherry-picking the best, deciding what is for now, what is worth waiting for.

Because if the flow of opportunities and initiatives becomes too much, you can share them with others on their brand-building journey. This is something I've enjoyed in recent years. I've shared speaking engagements, book signing events, and radio interviews. I no longer feel the need to accept everything, but then I am 40 years into my career. I enjoy helping others to shine.

The following chapters will help you secure the magnetic status that is within your grasp if you can commit your time – with my know-how – and your personal brand plan to guide you. You'll see that I've covered in detail how to approach and work with the media, including social media. This is something I consider essential for every person. No pass, I'm afraid! I then share my professional public speaking tips before talking about my BOSS approach so you can fill your next event.

Finally, if you're curious about writing a book, but are unsure where to start and are baffled by the publishing options, I hope my experience in all aspects of book writing and publishing inspires you to put pen to paper.

Don't wait for the ideal time to embark on this new and exciting aspect of your journey where you're turning plans into action. I know from running my own business, juggling book writing, and organising conferences that the ideal time rarely happens. Spend some time on your personal brand plan, have your 'Whys' close by, and dive in!

You should start to see a pattern forming as you appraise your list of activities. For example, if you're interested in running your own events, then public speaking and building media relations will be part of your plan because you want to fill spaces fast. If you want to write a book, you'll need to focus on public speaking, building media relations, and organising sell-out book signing events.

As I've mentioned before, it's natural for your planned activities to start joining up. One of the benefits of connection is that when people see you 'popping' up everywhere, their curiosity turns to a fear of missing out.

I hope you enjoy working on this aspect of your personal brand-building journey, and that before long you're reaping the rewards.

Being magnetic is magical!

CHAPTER 9

Read All About It!

How to secure substantial media coverage

"... sharing your wisdom to benefit others embeds your status as a person of influence."

When I was nearing the final draft of *You're the Best!*, I spent an afternoon with Mike Yorke, a golf professional and former client. I value Mike's opinion, so after we'd talked about my book, we settled down to chat about social media, especially the never-ending stream of content on all platforms. Mike had an interesting take that I agree with. He was pruning his list of connections on LinkedIn so he could see the posts that really mattered and comment on them. As he explained:

> "Nowadays, my feed is full of posts and pictures that are not relevant to me. They offer little value especially as a growing number are from people, selling their latest scheme. I want to find the hungry market that is aligned with what I offer and those that take a little longer to nurture but are worth the effort. These are the people I want to be in front of and having decent conversations with. I'm in danger of overlooking them because of the surrounding noise."

You may be feeling something similar, that you can't see your prospects because they're submerged under 'stuff' that's of little interest to you.

In this chapter, I'm taking you on a tour of how to build a magnetic personal brand by creating targeted, relevant, and rich content, both online and in print. Content that reaches the people that matter and that grabs their attention. Because if you want to reach out to the people you identified in your personal brand plan, then creating relevant content puts you in pole position of having decent conversations with them.

One carefully crafted article, a captivating press release, or an illuminating blog can portray you as a key person of influence. And if your content hits the sweet spot, it will be shared by some of your prospects to their contacts. The secret to resharing comes from creating exceptional content, not rehashing someone else's, or creating a poorly written piece as clickbait. People see through this.

What is the message I would like you to take from this chapter regarding your target audiences?

Inspire them and watch those barriers fall.

Be different by creating content that demonstrates you're authentic and magnetic and that you care about your readers. This is something I've accomplished with great success over many years. I've encouraged clients to do likewise. On the strength of one blog or article, one post on LinkedIn plus a subsequent conversation, I've secured public speaking engagements, sold many books, and gained new clients.

Where should you start on your content creation journey?

I begin by creating subject matter lists for blogs, articles, and press releases, drawing on the facets of my marketing experience with small businesses and, more recently, my expertise as an author of fiction books as well as non-fiction. The thread connecting everything I create is my willingness to share the best of my knowledge and experience.

Do the same! Draw on yours.

This generous approach will pay you back, just as it has me.

As you're creating your subject matter list, go back to your personal brand plan and your target audiences. What will they find useful and inspiring? What are the angles that will ensure topics are compelling and shareable?

If you can arrive at 12 subjects, you've enough content for a year, because within each category lies the potential for a series of articles and blogs. You can also repurpose and edit pieces, thereby giving them a second life. Batching content reduces feelings of overwhelm and improves consistency.

So you have your list of subject matter. What's next?

Create Your Boilerplate

Your boilerplate sits at the end of your piece. It's your reward for submitting unique, reader-relevant content. Around 100-125 words is ample to paint an appealing picture. Include links to pages and websites you would like readers to explore. If you're an author, include a link to your website and Amazon page. I'm always astonished when I read an article or blog and at the end, the contributor has not included any information about themselves, not even their contact details. Some editors and moderators may not allow a boilerplate, but most will.

As you can see in my first boilerplate, I focus on my business books because my content is about marketing for small businesses. My goal was for readers to enjoy my article and to buy a book. In the second, my focus was on promoting *The Boutique*, as it was featured in my monthly magazine column about personal development and wellbeing. I had the same end goals; reinforce my name as a person of influence and sell books. I change my boilerplates regularly, depending on what I want to promote. Sometimes, it's a book signing, a writing workshop, or a conference for small businesses, most recently one of those.

This is your personal space. It's prime real estate that promotes you as a person of influence. What do you want to promote? One of my clients promotes their free garden design service, another their HR power hour, another their latest online training events.

About Dee Blick

Dee is a Fellow of The Chartered Institute of Marketing, a #1 bestselling author of The 15 Essential Marketing Masterclasses for Your Small Business (Wiley), rated 'an excellent read' by The Sun, CityAM, Elite Business Magazine and winner of the Bookbag non-fiction book award. Endorsed by the CIM, The Ultimate Small Business Marketing

Book has sold 20,000+ copies and hit the Amazon charts at position 150, staying in the top 10 bestselling marketing books for five years. It was also a bestseller in China (CITIC Publishing). The Ultimate Guide to Writing and Marketing a Bestselling Book was listed in The Guardian newspaper's top 10 reads for entrepreneurs. You can contact Dee at XXXX

About Dee Blick

Dee is an international bestselling author of five books. Her latest book, The Boutique, is Dee's first work of fiction: nine short stories with the nine characters connected through the eclectic and stylish fashion shop that is The Boutique. It's when these special people venture beyond the doors that the real drama starts to unfold, culminating in unexpected plot twists. Gripping, poignant and powerful, The Boutique is the ultimate 'curl up with a coffee' read and fact-meeting-fiction book. Dee loves talking to her readers so get in touch if you've read any of her books. And check out the many five-star reviews on Amazon.

So you have your list of enticing content, your boilerplate is punchy and you're ready to start writing.

What's next?

Can you share some of this content in a series of press releases? This works if you have genuinely interesting news about your business, you're commenting on recent research, or what you're covering is topical within a target audience's sector. Magazines still appreciate press releases. Make sure yours is so beautifully written and reader relevant that an editor wants to publish it.

How To Write Press Releases That Are Published

I've collaborated with many editors in the last four decades on a broad range of publications, from health and wellbeing glossies to niche interest publications and single subject magazines aimed at professional tradespeople. I was chatting to an editor recently who told me he receives around 50 press releases every day. His finger hovers perilously close to the delete button.

You gain many credits in the personal brand building bank when your release features in a publication valued by your target audience. It's more powerful than an advert, so spend time creating something that an editor will appreciate because they are the person you must impress, followed by their readers.

Here's one of mine, published without alteration, for *Health Triangle Magazine*, a paid-subscription, high-profile, online magazine with a global audience.

It had significant online exposure. It featured twice on LinkedIn, as well as appearing on Facebook, on the publisher's website and within the magazine. I also shared it on LinkedIn and Facebook, publicly thanking the editor, which led to reshares. The editor appreciated the opportunity to promote their magazine to new and existing audiences. Of course, it also strengthened my name as a person of influence.

Press Release for Immediate Release, March 7

Award-Winning Writer Joins Health Triangle Magazine

Dee Blick, an international bestselling author, has joined Health Triangle Magazine, with a monthly column: 'Living Well with Dee.'

Commenting on this, Dee said: "I love the ethos of this magazine, with its focus on inspiring, empowering, and informing readers to make choices which support their optimum mental and physical wellbeing. So I was thrilled when Raphaela, the Creative Director of Health Triangle Magazine, gave me the opportunity to reveal some of the lessons I've learned in my 62 years of living. I'm a recovering alcoholic with 25 years of sobriety. This has really taken me on that road less travelled, with the emphasis on embracing a healthy and purposeful life – minus a mood-altering substance to navigate the way. In the coming months, I will share more in my column, including how I overcame the anxiety that gripped me for many years, how I (finally!) managed a chronic health condition with meditation, and the steps I've taken to realise a childhood ambition of writing books. I hope my column will inspire readers to meet challenges and opportunities with confidence, because I believe that each one of us has the most incredible potential and that we can accomplish so much more than we give ourselves credit for. Sometimes, all it takes is a little encouragement to shed our self-limiting beliefs."

"We are delighted to welcome Dee to our team of writers," said Raphaela. "I am sure that with her words she will touch the hearts and minds of our readers globally."

Ends

Top Tips on Writing Press Releases

1. Keep them concise. This one is 259 words. Resist the temptation to stray beyond 300 words.

2. Make it bespoke to the publication. The editor must grasp its relevance and reader appeal, aligned with the focus and tone of their publication.

3. When structuring your release, work on the principle of the inverted pyramid. The core information should appear as close to the beginning as possible. If your release is then cropped after a few paragraphs, you've still managed to paint a decent picture.

4. Follow the structure of: Who, What, How, When. Conclude with a memorable sentence or a quote. Ideally both.

5. What's the tangible hook you're serving up in the opening lines that will stop an editor in their tracks and grasp the relevance of your release to their readers? Draft it and polish it to perfection.

6. Don't sell your services. That's the job of your boilerplate.

7. Avoid unsubstantiated superlatives. Words such as 'unique,' 'brilliant,' 'best,' and 'innovative' are powerful words, yet often overused. Don't stray into style over substance. Editors receive endless releases, brimming with hype. They're summarily deleted.

8. Include facts, figures, and your reaction to research if this supports your content. Be strident with your opinions, especially when commenting on trends and market conditions, but avoid outright controversy which could jar with the editorial focus and tone of the publication.

9. Include comments to make it lively and relatable to readers. The editor could pull these out and enlarge them. A thought-provoking quote from you could be significantly enlarged when published.

10. Proofread your release to root out overuse of words and sloppy grammar. Allow a few hours between creation and checking, then read it through at least three times.

11. Underneath 'Ends,' include all your contact details within your boilerplate, leading with these. Some editors will phone, others will email, some will reach out on social media. Offer high-quality images but don't include them as you may overload their inbox!

12. If you're tight for time, create unique content for your favoured publication, followed by fresh content for others further down the line. Editors don't like seeing the same release in rival publications. They're unlikely to publish your content again if you do this.

13. You can, however, save time by modifying a release. Change it sufficiently to give it a new lease of life elsewhere. I usually change 60% of a release and I add in new speech comments. I create a new title and completely change the introductory few lines.

14. Thank the editor when they publish your release and you're likely to secure more coverage.

15. Share your press release in your social posts, linking to the publication which will give you extra brownie points.

Sharing Your Influencer Status in Articles and Blogs

If press releases are perfect for news, views, and insights, how can you illuminate your personal brand with the same audiences? Because sharing your wisdom to benefit others embeds your status as a person of influence.

An easy first touchpoint is social media. Further into this chapter, I'm joined by Michelle Betts and Debbie Gilbert, sharing tips on how you can use social media to build your authentic and magnetic personal brand. Notwithstanding this, a well-stocked, personality-driven LinkedIn page works as your brand ambassador when an editor is doing their homework on you. This has been the case with Guy Watts, the managing director of Architectural Plants.

If, however, you want more than just social sharing – specifically, you want to reach out to your target audiences, sharing tips, wisdom, and know-how – then before you start, you must do some research into what they read. It's time to revisit your personal brand plan where you made a note of these audiences.

Which publications, blogs, and forums should be at the top of your list for featuring your content because they're supported by your audiences? Searching online should deliver the names and titles you're looking for. Social media is handy for locating editors and journalists. There will be an overlap with the publications you select for your press releases. It's not unusual to have a press release and an article in the same magazine if you've built a relationship with the editor.

Online publications and blogs must feed their readers regularly with fresh new content, so they're more likely to include your releases and content than a printed publication. Magazines targeted at professional tradespeople are easier to secure coverage than glossy magazines aimed at consumers. The latter is possible, but it can take several attempts to crack them. Later in the chapter, I share how I managed to do this for a client, with incredible results. You can copy this approach because all it takes is a mobile phone and a charming message.

Compose your list of publications and blogs, deciding on the ones you will initially target. Start small when you begin pitching, especially if you're venturing into uncharted territory. Having one editor happy to include you as a regular contributor is a great start, as is one blog. You can build on this.

Creative Ways To Share Rich and Relevant Content

Don't make the task of contributing content one that you dread because it takes too much time and energy. You want to make it easy for an editor to say yes and for you to write.

Here are some of the most popular ways I share my expertise through the written word for magazines and blogs in print and online. I've included formats that are easy for you to use. They're timeless, as popular now as they were when I started writing, way too many years ago!

Questions and Answers – 3, 5, 7

Start with a short introduction, then lead into the questions, with a summary as your conclusion. Questions must be genuine, not a thinly veiled attempt to sell your services. Your boilerplate is the reward. I have found these to be popular when I am writing about marketing; for example, the key questions small businesses ask me about a specific marketing subject. This format extends to all topics and sectors.

Top Tips 3, 5, 7, 10, 13

Again, write a short introduction to explain why you're sharing these tips, with a few sentences as your conclusion. Top tips remain a powerful format to share bite-sized wisdom. They're also perfect for spreading over three consecutive features. Just let readers know what to expect and when. By sharing your wisdom in this way, your authenticity and influencer status shines through. Sharing tips with lessons learned makes you memorable and relatable.

You can share your content under the banner of tips, strategies, approaches, winning ways, whatever you feel will hit the sweet spot with the editor and their readers. Keep your focus on helping, inspiring and entertaining readers.

At the end of this chapter, I've included two of my articles featuring top tips.

Customer Case Studies

One article that includes three customer case studies, with an introduction and a summary, makes for an interesting piece. My format for each individual case study within the article is easy to follow. I describe the needs of the customer, followed by how we solved/met these needs. I save any WOWs for the last few lines. I often include a comment from the customer because this will sometimes be displayed prominently in the published piece.

Commenting on Sector-Specific Research

Editors appreciate contributors that are willing to offer thoughtful responses to research that is relevant to their sector. Here's the headline and introduction to an article that I anchored in research, which was relevant to my client, Kalimex. I used this to then shift the focus onto the premium quality products Kalimex sells to garages, attributing the comments within the article to Mike Schlup, Managing Director. You may recognise Mike's name; he wrote the foreword to this book.

> ### *Aftermarket Survey Reveals Opportunities for Garages to Upsell*
>
> *A survey by Castrol has revealed garages are missing opportunities to offer high-quality consumables alongside a vehicle service, with 5 out of every 10 motorists saying they would be 'happy for their workshop to upsell more expensive, premium-quality consumables if the benefits were explained to them.' Commenting on this research, Mike Schlup, MD of Kalimex, said…*

Topical Insights

What is topical in the sector you're looking to target that you can comment on with your thoughtful and interesting insights? For example, when I'm writing about mental health, I will research the current conversations around it and reflect on these in my piece.

Interview a Thought Leader From Your Target Audience's Sector

Interviewing an interesting person is another popular way of gaining exposure for you and your interviewee. Make your interview easy to compose with a simple question-and-answer format, if writing a flowing narrative appears daunting or time-consuming. Six interesting questions is ample. The interview doesn't have to be face-to-face. Your interviewee may prefer to receive questions in writing or to be interviewed on Zoom. The latter gives you the option of sharing the recorded interview and writing it up. I've secured coverage in prestigious magazines simply by interviewing a client or a thought leader. My reward is being named as the interviewer in the sub-headline and being mentioned on the contents page, often with my photo. You can see my interview with Janine Lowe on page 174 as an example of how I did this technique.

Book Review

Can you review a book that readers will be interested in? For example, I recently reviewed *Feng Shui Your Way to Abundance* by Janine Lowe for *Health Triangle Magazine*. You can achieve your goal of securing coverage by helping others to share the spotlight.

I hope these suggestions have inspired you to start writing. The next step: how to ensure your great content finds its intended home.

Pitching for Cover: Charm the Editor First

I begin by ensuring I'm familiar with the publication or the blog, including their contributors. I don't want to overlap or tread on anyone's toes.

I then decide what I can add that is interesting to readers and that complements the style, tone of voice, and focus of the publication or blog. I go back to my list of ideas to decide what I think could work. It might be a one-off article, a column, top tips, lessons learned in life or business, or a considered opinion on what's happening in the sector.

I contact the editor on social media by sending a personal message. Sometimes, this works; other times, I draw a blank.

Undeterred, I send a concise but friendly email with my suggestion as a potential contributor of content. I hope you find the following email to the editor of *Health Triangle Magazine* useful, whether you're pitching for a column, a solo article, or are sending your press release and want to draw attention to it.

With this email, I didn't start by pitching for a regular column until the editor had praised my first article and I had demonstrated my commitment to delivering on my promises, including word count. The press release you saw earlier came after this email.

Follow my lead. Build trust, deliver to a high standard, and then go back with other ideas on a similar theme.

Hi Raphaela,

I hope my email finds you in wonderful spirits.

I would like to propose a new columnist for your magazine... Do bear with me whilst I explain more!

A few days ago, I received a lovely email from the Women's Institute inviting me to be their solo speaker at a literary event, with the aim of sharing my story and signing copies of The Boutique. The comment from the lady inviting me was that many of their members would resonate with my story of overcoming adversity and addiction, before writing a fiction book at the age of 62.

This got me thinking about your magazine and I have an idea for your consideration...

As a woman over 60 with a 40-year history of writing for magazines, blogs, and books, I know that I carry a strong and positive message to other women. I can encourage them to look after themselves, mind, body, and spirit. I have been told by many people on many occasions that I am a force for good, that I inspire people to dig deep, especially in business. I mentor women at no charge, specifically women that would never be able to afford my fees, and I use my platform as an author and businessperson to share a positive message. I look after myself with regards to my diet and my mental wellbeing, and I have 26 years of recovery. I have also managed to run a successful business on my terms, as an ethical, people-first woman.

I could write a column for your magazine focusing on the mind, body, and spirit aspect of how I have lived my life, the changes I've had to make, and how others can follow if they too are at a crossroads in life or are looking to make positive change without pills or quick short-term fixes.

My email went on to suggest the subject headlines for a column which is why it's always a good idea to have your subject matter lists beforehand. I'm now a monthly columnist for the magazine, and on the back of this, have secured book reviews and several radio interviews from their sister business, UK Health Radio.

Be Different – Send a Video Instead

Sometimes, an email will not work because there's little chance it will reach the editor. You'll only know this through trial and error. I worked with a client where I advised them instead to create a 90-second bespoke video to the editor and their magazine. My client was pinning his hopes on securing coverage in three glossy consumer magazines. A bold ambition!

In each video, recorded on his iPhone, my client introduced himself as the founder of a premium vegan skincare business. He suggested sending the editor a sample of their products. He went on to introduce his mum and partner because they worked in the business. They said hello and gave a brief demonstration of the products.

All three editors responded, asking for samples and offering free coverage, which exceeded even my expectations.

We did spend a day on the videos, staging the products, creating the perfect backdrop, and rehearsing the short scripts.

My client introduced himself in each video as follows.

> *"Hi [name of editor], I know you receive many press releases for [name of magazine] so I wanted to introduce my business and our award-winning vegan skincare products to you in this little video. I'd love to send you some samples, but first you need to know what we do and why! In this video, I will introduce you to my mum and partner as they work with me."*

Comments from the editors were that the video was a pleasant surprise, and that my client came across as authentic and charming and they loved the family aspect of the business.

This is proof that being authentic with a good product or service is sometimes enough to grab the attention of an editor. Had we tried to secure coverage with a press release, I doubt we would've succeeded. Be creative if an editor is hard to reach and you're confident a video is your silver bullet.

Be Sure To Share

Once you see your articles, tips and press releases published, it's natural to want more. Don't be afraid to go back to the editors you're building a relationship with to suggest a regular column and new features, just as I do. Remember to thank them each time and ensure that your submissions adhere to the agreed-upon word count and are delivered on time.

Don't stop at admiring your handiwork. Share it and continue to build on your authenticity and magnetism.

1. Include this content when pitching for new business.

2. Add a press section on your website, with the most recent content on the home page.

3. Use some of the most powerful pieces to create short video blogs, sharing your insights and referencing them as an anchor.

4.   When pitching for speaking engagements, bring your content into the discussions and email follow-ups so you appear even more impressive.

5.   Use it to pitch for regular columns and news to various publications. When an editor sees the quality of your published work, it is easy for them to say yes. Remember the rule of changing 60% of any existing content, including the headline, speech comments, and your introductory paragraph.

6.   Share on your social channels, with one-to-one targeting of those most likely to be swayed by what you've accomplished.

7.   Create a compilation of your content as an eBook or physical copy when you are exhibiting, training, pitching – any situation where this dose of creativity and flair will add value to your presentations, formal and informal. It carries clout.

8.   Talk about your coverage with peers, customers, influencers, prospects, and suppliers. You never know where your next lucky break is going to come from! You can be as broad brush as you are detailed.

9.   Track what resonates with readers so that you can focus your energies on what works.

A Word of Warning About Overusing ChatGPT Content

I was chatting to an editor about artificial intelligence (AI) and how it is being used in content creation. He told me he'd seen a sharp rise in articles and press releases that had clearly been created using AI, with little original input from the sender. He was not publishing these pieces. He cited two press releases from two different businesses with eerily similar wording and phrases.

Using AI for inspiration, which I advocate for, is vastly different from using AI to do your job. If you want to build strong media relationships but are planning on using content dependent on AI, you're unlikely to succeed. Overusing AI doesn't build strong brands. Your content should carry your brand DNA. AI has its place – and it can be incredibly useful in firing your imagination and providing useful steer when you're building your marketing and branding plans. Just don't use it lazily in place of your pen. You'll be caught out.

Three Pieces of My Content To Help You Write Yours

Example One: Long top tips, blog, 648 words.

I wrote this for a blue-chip brand. They paid me to write a high-profile monthly blog for 12 months. I hope you also find the subject matter useful.

The 13 Marketing Secrets of Successful Small Businesses

It's tempting to think successful small businesses have found something extraordinary in the marketing department, that they've discovered the marketing miracle at the end of the rainbow with their name on it.

The good news is that there isn't a marketing miracle you haven't yet found. Or at least that's my experience, having worked with hundreds of small businesses in the last 35 years.

Marketing-savvy small businesses do the following:

1. **They recognise that a great product or service is not enough to build a successful business,** *so they put marketing at the heart of their business, blocking out marketing time. They market in good times, despite being busy. They market in lean times, doubling down to keep the sales rolling in.*

2. **They wear many hats, but they know when it's time to drop the DIY approach and enlist the experts.** *I'm talking about the graphic designers who give their logo and communications impact and flair; the web designers who do likewise for their website; and the copywriters who help when they're full of ideas but find it challenging to put pen to paper.*

3. *They radiate enthusiasm and positivity and are always ready to do business.* They're natural connectors, looking for ways in which they can collaborate with talented folk that complement their skills. They're generous, referring good leads and business to others, knowing their generosity will have a karmic effect.

4. *They're clear about their offering.* Ask them what they do and, within a few sentences, you've grasped it, so much so that if you're in the market for what they offer, you're keen to learn more. They're big on benefits and they know what customers need and want.

5. *They keep an eye on competitors so they can learn and improve* but they always blaze their own trail.

6. *They make their marketing accountable.* They won't shrink from abandoning a marketing activity that's not worked, and they keep close tabs on the responses so their marketing does not drift.

7. *They look for ways to improve their products and services.* This ranges from the small tweaks that can be accomplished easily, to the intensive ones that have to be scheduled and budgeted for. Running parallel to this is their overwhelming desire to delight customers. They build their business around happy customers and never lose the personal touch.

8. *They're not content to remain in their comfort zone.* *They take calculated risks, establish bold goals, and invest in their personal development. It feels daunting, but they do it.*

9. *They invest time in their marketing plan before diving into marketing tactics.* *Consequently, they know who they want to reach and why. They know where they can locate their target audiences so they can successfully reach them. They build campaigns over a period to build trust and break down barriers. They focus on creating captivating, relevant, and attention-grabbing messages, wrapped up in appealing communications.*

10. *They recognise the value in traditional marketing as well as social media.* *Their choice of marketing tools and communications is determined by the preferences of their target audiences and not their prejudices. They embrace print and pixels!*

11. *They build on their influencer status, investing in their skills and broadening their knowledge.* *They share their expertise as a person of influence across many marketing platforms, from social media to blogging and speaking.*

12. *They have a heartbeat and a conscience.* *They actively seek ways in which they can support charities or special causes, and are keen to minimise their impact on the environment. They are always authentic.*

13. *Their business keeps them awake at night with excitement, sometimes fear. But they're resilient. When times are tough, instead of duvet diving, they double their efforts, bouncing back stronger and fitter.*

And, of course, they love what they do. Half measures avail them nothing!

Example Two: Concise, single topic tips, 442 words.

This was for a client that rents mailing lists to businesses. In a previous monthly blog, I explored several themes related to direct mail and mailing lists, each time with a single-topic focus. As advised earlier, before I start writing, I work on my subject matter list, which currently includes 12 topics, many of which are connected, with some forming a series of three.

4 Common Sense Direct Mail Tips

Before you think about picking up your pen or dipping into your budget, follow my four-step process to creating successful direct mailshots. I've been running income-generating direct mail campaigns for blue-chip brands and agile small businesses for decades. Follow my tips and you'll reap the rewards.

1. *Establish realistic objectives for your direct mail campaign. For example, suppose you're entering a market with competitors but are new to it. In that case, your goal should be to rapidly*

build awareness before moving to engaging on a one-to-one level with influencers, introducers, and prospects. With direct mail, you can also acquire an abundance of new customers at a low acquisition cost. If your aim is to continue selling your products or services in a mature market, where you have strong roots and a healthy customer base, direct mail is perfect tool for selling to more of the same customers. Information-rich communications with genuine offers underpinned by evident value will do the trick.

2. ***Be clear on brand positioning.*** *You must convey your brand personality and values within your mailshot. Can you tell your story so that people can see you have roots? You may offer products and services like those offered by other businesses. How you present your brand so that it has impact is crucial. When a person opens your mailshot, it should elicit a smile at the very least, a "Wow!" at the best. Fundamentally, its aim must be to make that person want to buy, enquire, or recommend.*

3. ***How can you demonstrate you are value focused?*** *The PIMS Forum (Profit Impact of Marketing Strategies) found that companies perceived by customers as giving value for money tend to be "infinitely more profitable than companies that don't focus on giving value." Within your mailshot, you must communicate how you deliver value. Don't overcomplicate.*

Can you share your value in three steps or a few sentences?

4. ***Make a list of everything you must do before starting.***

- *Do you need to buy or rent a list of cold prospects for one-time or multiple use?*

- *Have you researched your target audience sufficiently to understand the needs that will propel them to respond to your mailshot?*

- *Do you have the resources in-house to manage your campaign, from concept to mail-out, or will you need to use the enclosing and dispatch services of a fulfilment house?*

- *Are your team members poised for action? For example, have your account handlers or salespeople allocated time to follow up on the phone after the mailshots have been sent? Dig out that diary!*

I hope my advice has resonated with you…

Example Three: Interview with a businesswoman, under 550 words

I've used this simple format to interview many people of influence, from the founder of a local charity to a gold medal Olympian, and a well-known crime correspondent. Most interviews have been conducted over email, making them easy to arrange and complete. Janine was a speaker at the Brilliant & Bold conference I was organising. As part of our 'thank you' speaker package, I arranged interviews for every speaker with our media partner, Sussex Exclusive. It was great PR for Janine because the website and magazine has a huge following in the millions, and she was able to promote her book and varied services. Don't turn down an interview if you're offered one, and don't hesitate to suggest one: it can lead to other opportunities.

Coffee Catch-Up

Sussex Exclusive and Dee Blick catch up with Janine Lowe, author of Feng Shui Your Way to Abundance

How did your journey with Feng Shui begin?
Being intuitive is part of who I am. But back in the day, people didn't really know what to do with that. In fact, they'd often recoil, which made it lonely at times. Then, in my twenties, a dear friend, Lizetta, introduced me to Feng Shui... and honestly, it was like something clicked. At the same time, I was doing a photography course, focusing on buildings and suddenly, everything came together. My intuition, my love of spaces, and Feng Shui... it all aligned so naturally. I'd found the missing piece, and I've never looked back.

What inspired you to write Feng Shui Your Way to Abundance?

2020 completely changed how I worked. I couldn't see clients in person and for someone who's used to walking through homes, feeling the energy, and helping people shift it in real-time, it was a big adjustment.

So I thought, "What can I do to still support them?" That's when the idea came to me – I'd write a book that was simple, practical, and easy to follow. Something that would guide people to Feng Shui their own homes, even if I couldn't be there physically. I wanted it to feel like having me in the room with them, with warmth, encouragement, and real tools they could use straight away.

Where's the biggest demand for your Feng Shui expertise?

On the private side, I work with people seeking to bring harmony into their homes and manifest better love, health, and abundance. Commercially, there's growing demand from business owners: shops, spas, and offices looking to boost energy, flow, and profits through Feng Shui.

What gives you the most satisfaction?

Empowering people to shift their energy and bring abundance, balance, and joy into their lives… that's what lights me up.

You're a radio presenter for UK Health Radio, lifting the lid on Feng Shui.
I choose guests I find interesting and inspiring, because if they spark my curiosity, I know they'll spark my listeners' too. It's all about sharing conversations that uplift, inform, and empower people.

How do you use Feng Shui in your home?
I use all the core Feng Shui principles in my home and adjust them every year to align with the Flying Stars. Everything is placed with intention to invite happiness, wealth, and abundance. It's a living, breathing space that evolves with the positive energy I bring in.

How can readers access your expertise?
On my website, you'll find everything, from my Janine Lowe Feng Shui Academy, my books and podcast, to 1:1 Chinese Astrology readings, and, of course, you can book me to Feng Shui your home. Whether you prefer online, in person, or something in-between, pop over to www.janinelowe.co.uk

What does the future hold for you?
I'm writing my next book, Manifest Your Way to Abundance. I'll also be running workshops on how to get what you want right now, using a blend of Feng Shui, energy work, and practical manifestation tools. It's all about helping people step into their power and live with purpose.

Social Media and Personal Brand Building

It's easy to get drawn into social media, scrolling and reacting to amusing or touching posts. Before you know it, a few hours have gone by. However, if you're using social media to build your personal brand, this takes time and commitment. It's a different exercise from simply being present and checking in on your pages, chatting with friends and acquaintances. Before diving in and spending hours on social media with your business head on, you must ensure that your target audiences are also present on the platforms you frequent and that you can access them, either through distinct groups or in sufficient quantities, within your general following.

Be disciplined and set a time limit for social sharing so that you don't stray off-topic or lose focus. I've used LinkedIn and Facebook to promote my books, and it has been effective in generating interest and early sales, especially in the run-up to a book's publication. I share my writing progress, including images of the final manuscript, chapter headings, and the unboxing of the first delivery of a book, plus videos of my launches and details of upcoming events. I also share reviews – both the good and the negative ones – and I make a point of responding personally to every reader who contacts me.

I also promote my events by updating the businesses that are attending and the number of tickets remaining. Positive actions and engaging content can help build your personal brand on social media, but they must be factored into your overall personal brand plan. Social media may be crucial to your personal brand building, or it may be marginal. Your target audiences, and where they spend time together, hold the answer.

Don't lose sight of the fact that whether you're using social media to promote your business or not, people will find you and they will check out what you're saying and how you comment on other posts. They will also form an impression of the look and feel of your pages. Make sure that what they see and the impression they form is entirely consistent with the image you're looking to present as you build your personal brand. As I mentioned in Chapter 3, people will not draw a line between what you say as a businessperson and what you say in your free time when you're relaxed without a filter. Like it or not, with social media you're always on show.

This is what Michelle Betts, a respected social media consultant, has to say about using social media, followed by Debbie Gilbert, who runs popular LinkedIn training workshops.

Social Substance
by Michelle Betts

Social media changes constantly. One week, a trending sound is everywhere; the next, it's vanished. But beneath the surface-level trends are a few core things that really count. If you want to build a strong and authentic presence online, these are the six areas I encourage you to focus on:

1. ***Authenticity isn't a trend.*** *Being genuine online has never been more important. Whether*

you're a one-person business or part of a larger team, people want to know who you are and what defines your business. That means showing up with honesty, sharing behind-the-scenes moments, and being open about the journey. You don't need to reveal everything, but you do need to sound like yourself. Audiences connect with people, so be relatable, genuine, and inspiring.

2. **You don't need to post every day**. Quality will always beat quantity. A single post that makes people laugh, learn, or feel something is much more powerful than 10 posts that do nothing and are performative. Ask yourself whether each post serves a purpose. Does it add value, start a conversation, or reflect your brand in the right way? If not, it's better left out. Focus on consistency, something Dee spoke about in Chapter 3, rather than constant output.

3. **Community is more valuable than reach.** It's easy to get caught up in numbers, but followers are just a number unless they're engaged. The best results come from genuine interaction. Reply to comments. Ask questions. Be curious! Celebrate your customers. Social media should feel like a two-way conversation, not a one-way broadcast. If people feel seen and heard, they'll stick around and bring others with them.

4. **Video works (even if you're sick of hearing that!)**. Short-form video remains one of the

strongest ways to get attention and build trust. But here's the good news: it doesn't have to be slick. In fact, raw, relatable videos often perform better than the polished pros. You don't need studio lighting or a perfect script. Just talk to the camera as you would to a client. Be clear, be useful, and don't over-think it. This also works well in attracting the attention of an editor, as Dee shared earlier.

5. ***Keep an eye on the data, but don't obsess.*** Analytics can be helpful, but they're not the whole story. Not every great post goes viral; in fact, very few do, and not every viral post builds a business. Look at what's working, pay attention to patterns, but don't let the numbers stop you from experimenting. You're not trying to win the internet; you're trying to connect with the right people.

6. ***Done is better than perfect.*** This is the truth that no one wants to hear. Perfection is a brilliant excuse to delay. Great ideas often die in a drafts folder because someone was waiting for the perfect caption or the right lighting! Meanwhile, the people who are showing up regularly, flaws and all, are building momentum.

You don't need perfect. You need honest, helpful, human content… and you need to post it and engage when you get responses.

LinkedIn: Building Authenticity by Debbie Gilbert

Over the years, I've worked with thousands of people, helping them enhance and leverage their presence on LinkedIn. This platform is not just another social media outlet, but the best platform to build an authentic and magnetic brand, one that will empower you to reach new professional heights.

Many people put little thought into their LinkedIn profile and see it more as a box-filling exercise rather than the opportunity it is. You're listing yourself on the world's largest professional database. Therefore, care and consideration are paramount to leverage new clients from this platform. Here are some key considerations:

1. ***Your personal brand message.*** *Start by defining your personal brand message, which must be clear. When you complete your profile, take time to complete the 'About' section. This section is not just a space filler but a crucial part of your profile where you define what you do and stand for. Share your values, mission, and expertise. It must be clear, so people know who you help, how you help them, and why it matters. Your 'About' section should reflect this clearly and authentically, guiding your audience to understand your professional identity.*

2. ***Optimise your profile.*** *Your LinkedIn profile has one main aim: to attract people to connect with you! Ensure you use a professional, approachable profile photo, not one of you sitting on a beach with a cocktail! Use the profile banner with an image that aligns with your brand. Use the headline to detail the keywords around your business to help get your profile found by potential clients. Some people use sentences in their headlines, but this often gets cut off when you post, and if it doesn't have keywords, your profile is unlikely to be found in a search. I personally think keywords in your headline is more effective.*

3. ***Share your story.*** *People connect with people, not job titles. Share milestones, lessons learned, challenges you've overcome, and the 'Whys' behind your work. There is nothing more powerful in business than your story; it is a tool that can build trust and confidence in your audience. Share this in your 'About' section and when you post. Let your passion for your industry come across.*

4. ***Create value-driven content.*** *When you post, make it count. Share your knowledge and expertise. As you build your presence, you will notice that people will engage with helpful, relevant insights, industry news, or personal reflections. Ask questions, share tips, or offer advice that speaks directly to your audience's pain points and aspirations. Contrary to other*

LinkedIn experts, I don't think you need to post every day. Posting for posting sake won't get you more clients. It might even turn people off working with you! Quality over quantity gets the best results.

5. **Engage – genuinely.** Some of the biggest wins for my clients have been through their engagement. Comment thoughtfully on others' content, celebrate their victories, and respond to comments on your posts. LinkedIn rewards engagement, and so does your network.

6. **Be true to your voice.** To build your authenticity, use a consistent tone when you post. Ensure your visual style and messaging across your posts is consistent. Let your authentic personality shine and allow people to sense if you're bold, warm, quirky, or direct. You can build a picture of someone through their use of LinkedIn and enable people to understand you through your posts and comments.

7. **Leverage recommendations.** Request (and give) recommendations that reflect the impact of your work. These real-world endorsements enhance your credibility and trustworthiness. You must be a first degree to someone to ask for a recommendation. Ask people you have worked with, who can vouch for your work. These are incredibly powerful as digital proof, and you can repurpose them in your website and marketing materials.

8. ***Share the real moments.*** *Show the human side of your business. Whether it's a team win, a lesson learned, or a day-in-the-life moments, sharing this creates connection. Tag people you met or mention others in your posts — a thank you on LinkedIn can go a long way!*

9. ***Highlight wins.*** *Celebrate achievements; it's not bragging when shared with humility by focusing on the impact or what you learned, rather than pure self-promotion. One of the most commented posts I ever had was when I won a Stevie Award in New York!*

10. ***Keep evolving.*** *An authentic brand grows with you. Stay open to feedback, try new formats (video, polls, newsletters), and regularly reflect on what resonates with your audience. Check your analytics and track what is gaining engagement, shares, and follows.*

Case Study: Architectural Plants

I started working with Architectural Plants after Guy Watts, the managing director, asked me to provide ongoing media training and marketing mentoring for the marketing team.

The starting point was hosting half-day media events held at the nursery, giving journalists and editors the opportunity to experience the brand in all its vibrant glory. Jason Gilford, Head of Marketing, created a 12-month programme of events so that a journalist could commit to attending at least one of them. Guy spoke at every event. They have been a real success, attended by journalists and editors from some of the biggest publications, which cover garden design and maintenance.

As Jason explains:

> "We make a point of understanding the profile of each publication, the content they curate, and how we can add value. So when I'm sending an invitation to a media event, my message is personalised, and I follow up with a phone call and a confirmation email. We've found that small touches, such as collecting a journalist from the nearest train station and offering grazing boards from local artisan caterers, are really appreciated.
>
> We also provide journalists with ready-to-go content and images, which are perfect when they need to fill a space, and fast! Every month, we create new content that is topical and relevant to our brand. Events rank highly in our PR plan. This year, we attended the RHS Chelsea Flower Show, with a key media-focused position that was much more prominent than in previous years. It was a big investment, so we had to deliver significant exposure. We invited journalists, influencers, and editors, and ensured that on the official press day, we had an engaging, visual stand for photo opportunities, plus a colourful and interactive digital press pack. This documentation included a detailed explanation of our credentials as a genuinely sustainable business and a socially

responsible employer. With this meticulous approach to PR, we consistently achieve substantial coverage every month. It takes time but the payback has been fantastic. We're securing full pages of editorial in some of the biggest home and garden publications."

Guy's profile has blossomed in the last year, culminating in a 10-minute interview, which took place at the nursery in West Sussex. This was broadcast on BBC2 as part of the RHS Chelsea Flower Show coverage.

As Guy explains:

"I wanted to speak at the media events at our HQ so I could get to know every journalist and editor by name and build on my public speaking skills. At Dee's suggestion, I also revamped my LinkedIn profile, making it more human facing and personal to me, than just a signpost to our Architectural Plants' page, which it was before. This has helped in getting the attention of journalists and encouraging personal messaging. I'm also seeing a much better engagement with my posts and more invitations to connect with relevant people. One of my personal brand goals was to speak at high-profile events. Through one of our commercial customers, I had the opportunity to speak at the Ideal Home Exhibition, which gave me great exposure. The TV interview with the BBC has helped in building my status as a key person of influence, leading to many media and speaking opportunities. This has included being invited as a keynote speaker at Chichester Cathedral's Sponsors' Dinner for The Flower Festival in 2026. Previous speakers have included the author Kate Mosse and actor Hugh Bonneville, so I'm in illustrious company. This journey began with Dee encouraging me to build my personal brand alongside the business brand. The two are linked, with the net result that our business has benefited significantly, with more customers and more high-value connections, with introducers and influencers in garden design and horticulture."

Special Brand Promotion Focus

Producing Your Own Magazine: The Ultimate Media Communication

As you have seen, securing coverage in publications is a powerful way to promote your personal brand and your business brand. Why not go one step further and produce a publication where you get to choose the content and to display every facet of your brand?

This is not as onerous or expensive as you may think. It is certainly worth your exploration. A magazine is also the antidote to a brochure which can be one-dimensional and dates quickly. I've produced several high-quality, low-cost magazines for clients, including global brands looking to reach out to their international distributors.

Your business is neither too small nor too big to leverage the power of a magazine.

It can generate business through effective targeting of existing customers and cold prospects. It can also keep non-fee earning stakeholders, such as influencers and introducers, engaged with your brand.

A magazine is a superb way of highlighting you as a genuine person of influence, alongside your business. You get to choose the content and focus.

You can keep costs low with online distribution only or have printed copies. I do both for maximum reach and impact.

Here are my top tips for producing a magazine that will promote the absolute best of your personal brand and business brand.

1. **Be clear about your reasons.** If your marketing communications have become lacklustre, a magazine will take your brand to an enhanced level of status. If you must become more creative when targeting people and standing out from competitors, a magazine really ticks this box.

2. **Content and images are crucial so plan yours upfront.** A magazine is no excuse for indulging you and your business, with unrelenting promotional content and images appropriate for personal sharing only. Approach yours through the eyes of those you want to reach. What would they find interesting and of value? What must they know about you and your brand to form a "Wow!" impression? Which images need including so they augment the written content? Is a photographer required? They will tick several boxes, from taking images of you and your team,

to photographing products and portraying creative images of your logo. Reduce your reliance on the stock images you can readily access but that are seen frequently.

3. **Rich and relevant content is crucial.** You need a palette of interesting articles, tips, and features ranging in size from 400 words for a single page with images, to 1,200 words for a three-page feature. I hope the following inspires you from a magazine, *JLM Drive*, which I produced for several years for JLM Lubricants. Workshop technicians and businesses selling to them were the main target audiences. We also wanted to strengthen connections with distributors in over 40 countries.

For the sixth edition, content included:

- An interview with the founder, Gilbert Groot. Because an interview with Gilbert featured in every magazine, I had to convey him as a global person of influence with his finger on the pulse of the latest trends and research. These were double-page features, making Gilbert more accessible and indeed captivating to a bigger audience.

- The JLM business opportunity for new distributors.

- Product spotlights – a different focus in every magazine on workshop hero products.

- Several features on global trends in the automotive industry, covering sustainability and the movement of Products over Parts and Repair over Replace.

- Commentary on a specific survey, which had an international reach.

- Details of JLM Lubricants' latest campaign.

- An interview with a team member. This was a regular feature.

- A feature on specific trends in several territories.

- Reasons why top tier technicians were using JLM products, including an interview with a leading technician to underpin these.

- The current product catalogue. The magazine also served as a product brochure, making it indispensable to resellers.

- A contents page with professional images of technicians, products, and events, with the aim of drawing the reader in to discover more.

- A welcome page from Gilbert, highlighting some of the content and reinforcing the brand story. Another powerful way of positioning him as an authentic and magnetic leader.

This magazine was 60 pages, including the cover. The first issue was 36 pages.

1. Looking at this list, what inspires you? Could you share some of the benefits of specific products and

services? Could you use the top tips format, questions and answers, case studies, and press releases discussed earlier in the chapter to produce articles? What is happening in your sector – locally, nationally, and globally – that you could share in the format of an interview, thereby displaying your influencer status? Could you include a guest writer, such as a person that complements your expertise? I've always included these, briefing them to subtly endorse the business founder, alongside sharing their expertise. Could you share your updated brand story, your commitment to sustainability, and snippets of events you've spoken at?

2.   Create a flat plan of content with the word count and images required.

3.   Have a catchy name. This is where AI can help. It must be relevant to your business and resonate with your audiences.

4.   Use professionals! I work with designers to produce clients' magazines. Your business brand and personal brand deserves a compelling, easy-to-read, professional format. Your magazine may last a year and reach thousands of readers. Avoid cost-cutting with DIY design. You may also want to enlist a copywriter and a proofreader to ensure your magazine does not bear the bruises of grammatical errors, poor punctuation, and unwieldy sentences!

5.   Promote it before, during, and after production. Distributors used *JLM Drive* in many ways, including

VIP direct mail campaigns, giving copies to journalists and visitors when exhibiting and promoting online. When distributors were sending copies to resellers such as motor factors, they included my top tips on how they could use *JLM Drive* to stimulate more sales. For distributors, I ran marketing masterclasses so they were primed for promotion.

6. Promote your personal brand. Your magazine is a powerful tool when pitching for public speaking engagements, talking to editors and journalists, and promoting your latest event. It's perfect if you've written a book, because you can include excerpts and reviews to encourage more sales.

Produced with care and lavished with attention, your magazine will convey your standing as the magnetic, talented, and impressive founder of an exciting and laudable business.

Your Takeaways

1. Focus on creating content that's aligned with your target audiences and that conveys your influencer status.

2. Inspire your target audiences with timely and topical content so they want to continue the conversation with you.

3. Choose 12 subjects that can spawn a significant batch of content, and you won't feel overwhelmed.

4. Your boilerplate is the reward for creating rich and relevant pitch-free content.

5. Press releases are powerful. Ensure they're concise and interesting with every sentence checked before sending to the editor.

6. Be imaginative when pitching for cover and make life easier using tried-and-tested formats instead of a flowing narrative.

7. Promote every bit of coverage through all your communication channels to gain the most benefit.

8. Build relationships with journalists and editors. Always be prepared to do something imaginative and enticing to grab their attention.

9. Would a magazine take your personal brand and business brand promotion to a whole new level of influence and magnetism?

CHAPTER 10

Speak Up!

How to be an authentic and magnetic speaker

"Keep it simple.
Talk about what ignites
you, inspires you and
that you know inside out.
This is more than enough
just as you are more
than enough!"

If you'd told me 20 years ago that one day I would be speaking to large audiences with no prompts to support me, and I would be paid for the pleasure, I would have dismissed it as laughable. How could I, a person who approached local speaking engagements with a fear I'd fall apart, move into a space reserved for the supremely confident few?

Yet this is what happened. I went from delivering my 60-second elevator pitch at the business networking membership group BNI, to speaking at local business events, and then becoming a professional, paid speaker.

How did I manage to pull it off?

I share how in this chapter. There are many books on public speaking that will take you through the entire process, so if you're new to it, make sure you're grounded in the basics and consider some public speaking training. Perhaps you would rather join a local speaker group. In this chapter, I share the tips and techniques that have contributed to my transformation from being fearful of speaking, to becoming a confident and relaxed paid speaker. I also reveal how I've managed when things haven't gone to plan and how I negotiate higher-than-average fees.

I've also invited two speakers I respect, Ted Gooda and Stefan Thomas, to share their tips on public speaking. I hope that by the time you reach the end of this chapter, you will feel more confident about public speaking, be willing to give it a try, and understand the role it plays in building your personal brand.

In today's fast-paced and frenetic world where we communicate through so many channels, public speaking is no longer restricted to standing on a stage and addressing an audience. It comes in many forms, from participating in online discussions at events and delivering workshops, to contributing to forums, discussion groups, and podcasts. However, presenting live on a stage is what seems to evoke the most fear in us so my tips are focused on this. If you can master talking to a live audience, then other presenting scenarios are a breeze by comparison.

The key to success lies in being authentic, approachable, and relatable, not being a carbon copy of another speaker. Being the best version of you is enough to build a firm foundation for success. I'm sure you're familiar with this theme by now as I return to it frequently! So here are my top tips.

1. **Recognise the part public speaking plays in building your personal brand.**

    If you're fearful of public speaking, you're in the majority, so when you decide to act and share your wisdom on a stage no less, you're in the minority. Now you're really standing out among your peers and competitors as an effortless, engaging speaker. You also stand out with your audiences as a person to be admired and respected.

    When the global publisher Wiley offered a publishing deal for my third book, the marketing team made it clear that I had to be comfortable with public speaking, including at some of the biggest business events in the UK. I had a compelling reason to overcome my fear and dive in! But fear aside, I could see how being on a stage as a headline speaker brought many benefits. For just one of these shows, I would appear in the event magazine with a write-up about my talk, alongside my photo.

    On the day, my name and image would feature on the keynote speaker posters. The organisers would promote me before, during, and after the event on their social channels to thousands of followers. This would encourage delegates to discuss me, attend my talk, and purchase a copy of my book at my publisher's stand.

    When I rocked up on the day, there were other benefits I had not appreciated. For example, by the end of my first talk, my book had risen to the top of the bestseller list and I was approached by several people from the audience, inviting me to speak at their events. Whether you've written a book or not, public speaking will help you to build your name as a genuine person of influence with a ripple effect that reaches your business.

2. **Recognise fear and swat it before you perform.**
    Public speaking is up there with our most dreaded fears, so we either cave in and risk delivering a poor performance, or we take it by the scruff of the neck and address it. In Chapter 5, I shared how I've overcome fear of failure in general, but in the minutes before I'm called to the stage, my anxiety can be at risk of overload; if I don't manage it, that is. In this time, I have learned to meditate by focusing on my breathing and repeatedly telling myself that I'm more than good enough to deliver, that I have earned the right to speak. In addition to giving myself permission to fail, I also give myself permission to be successful, and I allow the latter thought to prevail.

    Once I start speaking, I turn my attention like a megawatt beam directly onto my audience. This is not the time for self-indulging with negative emotions. I remind myself that I'm sharing useful information and insights with these people. They've given up their time to hear me speak so I owe it to them to give it my best shot. The Women's Institute has recently accepted me as a speaker after a nerve-wracking audition process. The structure of each event often entails me sitting patiently for up to 30 minutes before I'm announced. I spend this time focusing on my breathing and paying close attention to the surroundings. I can report that so far, I haven't fallen apart, but if I do, I'll get over it! I usually start my talk feeling calm and grateful for the opportunity. When I shift into a grateful mindset, it is a sign that my mental preparation has worked.

3. **Be authentic and move within your circle of power.**

I've attended talks where the speaker has floundered because they've tangled themselves in knots over their subject matter. Either they had too much to say and not enough time in which to say it, or they'd strayed into territory outside of their expertise. If you want the peace of mind that comes with being authentic when you are on that stage, avoid talking about subjects that you know little about. And know when to stop when it comes your content. Less is most definitely more. Audience members are evaluating you on both your style of presenting and your content. For a talk of say 30 minutes, sharing six tips is better than sharing 20. If you opt for the latter, you risk galloping to the finish line, aware that time is running out and you've barely made a dent in what you planned on saying.

Bring your audience onside when you introduce yourself, sharing elements of your story including how you've overcome barriers, made mistakes and learned from them. If your audience can identify with you before you've really got stuck into your talk, all the signs are good. Then focus on keeping it simple. Talking about what ignites you, and that will inspire your audience. This is more than enough just as you are more than enough!

4.   Reduce rather than remove your reliance on notes.
Today when I'm speaking, I don't use notes. It has, however, taken me several years to reach this stage. If you're considering going without notes, practise your talk unaided several times and see how it feels. There's no shame in using notes but remember they're just that – small aids to help you remember what you're going to say. Several years ago when I attended a conference, a speaker began her talk by telling us she had 38 slides to work through. And she was not joking, although by the time she had reached slide 24, her allotted time had ended. We were thankfully spared 14 further slides of illegible text. Audience members having to strain their eyes to read your detailed slides whilst trying to pay attention to what you're saying does not make for a magnetic performance. For a 30-minute talk, try to get by with a few slides if you're using them instead of notes. There's a growing trend of speakers using their mobile. However, if you're straining to read the small screen, you're undermining what could be a magnetic performance. I've also attended conferences where the speakers who were due to speak before me had to abandon their slides due to technical difficulties. Their Plan B was to panic and shorten their talks. The less reliant you are on prompts, the better. Go at your pace with the goal that, one day, you may not need them at all.

5.   It's a performance so add a touch of theatre.
Adding a touch of theatre was a game-changer for me, when I realised I could step into the shoes of an actor

and deliver my best performance and to entertain my audience. This may seem at odds with being authentic, but it isn't. You're tasked with entertaining your audience. This means stepping up and delivering your talk in a way that inspires them and makes them want to continue listening to the last sentence. You're not chatting to these people as you would a friend over coffee. However, when you're talking to an audience, you must accomplish the delicate balancing act of appearing relaxed and confident, with a dash of theatre to be memorable. So as I step onto the stage, I imagine that I'm an actor about to deliver my finest performance to a hushed audience. I pay close attention to my voice because it's a powerful asset when used effectively. I have a natural tendency to rush when talking so instead, I pause. Sometimes, this is used for dramatic effect, especially when I'm making a point that warrants special attention. Before starting a new sentence, I pause and then emphasise the first few words. I stand in a relaxed manner with my knees slightly bent, looking around the room, taking in the audience and smiling. This voice craft alone helps me remain calm and focused.

Here's what Ted Gooda, actor and bestselling author, has to say on the subject. I asked Ted to share some of her public speaking tips, because when she speaks, the audience listens.

"Public speaking terrified me. I was horribly self-conscious and couldn't talk 'naturally'. If I had to stand up in front of more than half a dozen people, my voice would become very high-pitched and shake like Larry the Lamb. I worried that people would laugh at me. Yet, as an actor, I feel confident standing on stage in front of hundreds of people, especially if they're laughing and engaged. I realised that I had no confidence in speaking as myself – only when I was pretending to be someone else and I'd learnt the lines.

So when I was first speaking at conferences, I began by writing a 'script' which meant I was well prepared. Inhabiting a role meant that I had to consider posture. A character who was confident in their subject matter would assume more of a power pose than me. I could mimic that, even if I didn't feel it myself. Doing voice work for the stage taught me that breathing from the diaphragm is key to learning how to project. It also lowers the pitch and increases the stability of my voice – so no more Larry the Lamb. I tried to include a joke near the start, usually at my own expense, because that gets an audience on side. Each time I forced myself to do public speaking, I became more confident and closer to being me rather than a character. These days, I no longer have that crippling fear of public speaking, no matter how big the audience, and I no longer need a script. But I wouldn't have believed that if you'd told me that even a decade ago."

6.   **When things go wrong, dig deep.**

Because I'm not reliant on prompts when speaking, it reduces the risk of what can go wrong. However, one experience at an event really threw me. The speaker scheduled to follow my talk cancelled. The first I was aware of this was when the organiser asked, as I was about to step on the stage, if I would extend my talk from 30 minutes to 50 minutes. I did not have 20 minutes of extra content up my sleeve, but I couldn't say no. So I involved the audience by asking questions that were related to my subject matter as I moved through my talk, pausing before asking each question, and then offering feedback on the answers. I used several minutes towards the end to explore one of the subjects in more detail, inviting the audience to share their thoughts on this. You may find yourself in a similar situation, so be mentally prepared. It's at times like this that you realise you're more capable and resilient than you could ever have imagined.

The unexpected behaviour of others may throw you off guard. I remember speaking at a conference to the franchisees of a global brand. The franchisor had previously seen me in action at a similar event, so they knew what to expect. Immediately after my talk, the sales manager thanked me, saying, "That was an interesting talk, Dee. But did I learn anything new from it? Probably not." Thankfully, the feedback from the franchisees in the lunch break told a different story. But his comments, delivered in the full glare of the audience, did sting for a while.

What happens if you find yourself having a crisis of confidence during your talk? This happened to me in front of an audience of 200 people. Ten minutes into my talk, my mind went completely blank; I froze and my mouth was so dry that I felt panicky. I paused for a few seconds, taking small sips of water to calm my nerves. Instead of floundering for what to say, I told the audience that I would expand on my previous point as it warranted further explanation. Then it was back to the performance. I remember thinking that I had not made a 500-mile round trip to return home without a fee because I had fallen apart! This practical assessment of the situation helped me get back on track. It lasted all of 30 seconds, but it felt like an eternity! In the break, the organiser told me that my presentation was one of the best he'd heard. This feedback made me realise that what goes on in our mind is not what we convey when speaking. After this experience, I felt shaken for a while so I had to remind myself that most speakers experience memory blank and that it's not the end of the world. It meant going back to the drawing board, addressing fear and cutting myself some slack.

The next time you're at an event, pay close attention to how the speakers manage glitches, personal or otherwise. We all have them. It's not the end of the world. It's human nature to make the occasional mistake in amongst our brilliant and authentic delivery! You're not a robot so be kind to yourself if a few things don't go to plan, and pat yourself on the back for holding it together so well.

7. **Find a local speaker group so you can hone your craft and build your confidence.**

We have a speaker group in my hometown which meets twice a month. The collective goal is to remove the fear from public speaking by giving people the opportunity to practise in a safe, non-judgemental setting. If you're new to speaking or would like to step up and start charging, I encourage you to join something similar. Then, when you do start pitching for and accepting speaking engagements, you will no longer feel like a learner driver! And you get to practise your material.

8. Gratitude is the attitude.

Instead of approaching public speaking with customary dread, try and reframe it as life affirming. You're doing something authentically with real flair and talent. This is going to put you on the road to building your personal brand. It is to be enjoyed, not endured. And you're in a privileged position to be given an audience that wants to see you in action. Make your audience the hero and be grateful for the opportunities that will inevitably come your way. When you're surrounded by people after your talk, keen to chat and tell you how you inspired them, you'll wonder why you felt so fearful. But take each talk as it comes and always be kind to yourself. You're doing something that few have the courage to take on with any conviction. When reflecting on an event, consider all the lovely, relatable human touches you incorporated into your talk. And if you can do better next time, remind yourself that you're a work in progress, just as we all are! Approach any further learning with curiosity and positive energy.

9. How to get paid for public speaking.

Before I stepped into the shoes of becoming a professional speaker and paid for my appearances, my approach was to hone my craft through plenty of practice. I also sharpened my subject matter, usually structuring my talks into a top tips format. And I wrote a book. Without a doubt, writing books has helped me secure dozens of paid engagements. However, I know many speakers that have not written a book and they are in demand, so don't be deterred if you have no intention of writing one. As I mentioned in Chapter 1, I had a lucky break when John Acton discovered me through my first book. After that engagement, I had a few months of intensive practice, which was fortuitous as I seemed to pick up many paid bookings. These included speaking at conferences organised by membership associations, global brands, and professional bodies. Knowing what to charge for your speaking is not an exact science. If you quote a figure outside of an organiser's budget, they will tell you. This happened to me once, but when I pointed out the extra touches I was willing to bring to the event, they found more budget and accepted my fee.

How did I work out my fees for speaking? I simply asked other professional speakers what they were charging and positioned mine at the higher end of the scale. How do I ensure that organisers appreciate the value I bring to their event, because this is crucial if they are to agree to my fee? I make a point of talking at length with the person responsible for booking the speakers. This interaction builds on a fledgling relationship, and it ensures I only accept an engagement if I'm confident I can meet their needs and it feels right. I have turned down events when it was clear that I was not the right fit. For some,

I did not identify with their brand values. Sadly, I had to turn down an event in Alberta, Canada due to ill health, but I did speak online at a conference in Osaka, which was exciting, if a little unnerving because the subtitles were out of sync with what I was saying. I had to really focus on my subject matter rather than reading the subtitles.

What are the extra touches you can bring to an event, which justifies a fair fee or a higher-than-average one? If you've written a book, then a book signing is usually well received. If not, consider a meet and greet before your talk; a nicely written summary of your talk, in print or online; offering to be part of any judging panel or expert panel; or, offering a 'clinic' for attendees to book on after your talk. These extras are useful when you're speaking at a two-day event and the organisers must offer an interesting and varied programme. Be creative. Offer to over-deliver and the organiser will not quibble with your fees. However, make sure that your expenses are covered and they are on top of your speaker fee. I had my fingers burned once when an organiser told me they had assumed my speaker fee included all my expenses. After that, I made sure my emails detailed travel, hotel and subsistence expenses, and were agreed by the organiser.

10. Shout loud!

Promote your elevated status as a professional speaker on your website, on social media, and in your content. When a person is looking for a professional speaker, they can see that you're a person of influence, worthy of consideration. Have video content showing you in action. Better still, have a compilation video of several talks. You can send this as proof of concept when a person enquires about you speaking at their event. Ask the organisers for feedback and add this to your speaker portfolio. These small touches add up and will help you secure more paid engagements.

I would like to conclude this chapter with some inspiring advice from the number one bestselling author and professional speaker, Stefan Thomas, on how he began public speaking, the tips that help him to relax, and why he channels his inner rock star!

"When I first started attending networking events and business shows, they always had one thing in common. There were these amazing, God-like beings described as 'guest speakers' – and I was utterly in awe of them. Because my thought process went, 'If these folk had been invited to speak at the event, they must be at the top of their game. They must be THE expert to be standing up at the front of the room sharing their wisdom with us.' And then I realised you could just ask and be that person at the front of the room. So over the next few years, that's what I did. Any event which would have me, I would drive there and speak! After a few hundred events, and several thousand miles on the road, someone asked me how much I would charge to speak at their conference – and I became a professional speaker!

At first, I was trying to emulate other speakers I admired. I would copy their tone of voice, their body language, and try to be a carbon copy of them on stage. But the more confident I became, the more I started relaxing into me, and the more people reacted positively to the real 'me' on stage.

For sure, I still lean into the public speaking training I've paid for over the years, but these days I turn up on stage as the same person you see off stage, just a slightly 'bigger' version of me. The tips I practise every time are as follows.

Immediately before I go on stage, I find a quiet place in the venue (which is often a toilet!) to sit down and relax. I take control of my breathing, shut my eyes, and imagine myself at my most confident. I vividly remember times when I was confident on stage, and picture myself coming onto stage with a huge smile on my face, feeling the best I've ever felt. Once I'm there in front of the audience, I can be a bigger version of myself. My body language and gestures can be much more exaggerated than if I were standing talking to you one-to-one. Everything from hand gestures to pauses can be bigger on stage, and I use those exaggerations to make important points, or help jokes to 'land'.

Being me on stage, and having people message me afterwards to tell me they really derived value from what I said, still gives me the same buzz it gave me when I started.

And I get the chance to be the rock star I never was."

Your Takeaways

1.   Showing up as relatable, warm, and authentic is the foundation upon which great speakers are born.

2.   Public speaking will build your name as an authentic and magnetic person of influence.

3.   It's natural to feel fearful in the build-up to a talk so have your anxiety-busting techniques on standby.

4.   Bring your audience onside at the outset by sharing your story, the mistakes you made, and how you overcame them.

5.   Don't abandon prompts, but practise using them so they don't distract from your presentation.

6.   If you make a mistake, remind yourself you're human. Have a recovery plan to get back on track.

7.   When you're confident you can charge, factor in added value so an organiser is happy to pay your fee.

CHAPTER 11

Planning the Perfect Packed-Out Event

How to leverage the BOSS

"When you want people to attend your event, sending charming personal messages that pique curiosity and instil FOMO is the best way to sell most of your tickets."

When I was chatting with my brother, Drew, about my latest conference for small businesses, which sold out in days, he suggested I include my know-how in this book. I responded that my approach was common sense, only to be told the only reason I was saying this was because I've been staging sell-out events for decades. He proceeded to rattle off several events he had attended that were far from full as proof that my common sense is not shared. I had to take the pill I prescribe for others!

So you have my brother to thank for this chapter!

If events are on your radar, I hope you find my tips useful, and not just in selling tickets but in creating an event that's a tribute to your authentic and magnetic personal brand. Staging an event will undoubtedly enhance your standing as a person of influence, especially if you can also be a keynote speaker. What's more, if you get the formula right, you can generate new revenue streams.

Over the last 40 years, I've created numerous successful events for my business and several clients. Most of these events were chargeable, including mine, except for the online marketing masterclasses I offered to small businesses during the Covid period.

Here's a summary of the most popular events I've played a key part in creating, including producing the original concepts. I hope this inspires you to organise your own. Why not start with a list of the events that appeal to you and whittle down to the top three?

For My Business

1. Several two-hour, evening marketing masterclasses. I launched these in quick succession. Subjects included marketing planning, copywriting, and direct mail. Once I had sold all the tickets for the first event, it was easy to fill the places on the others. Many delegates rebooked and recommended them to their friends, as well as small businesses.

2. Three full-day marketing masterclasses were held following a similar format to the evening masterclasses, but with more content and networking opportunities. I also brought in a guest speaker to add variety to my presentations. All places sold out. I used these events to build my VIP early bird list for my conference, which took place several months after the last masterclass.

3. A full-day marketing conference. I organised this as a blueprint to show others how to sell out their

events. I also wanted to build on my reputation as a bestselling author. I secured sponsors, exhibitors, and keynote speakers. One hundred and fifty people attended, and the event sold out in four weeks. The event was highly profitable as the exhibitors and sponsors covered most of the costs.

4. A full-day non-profit business conference to support a charity I'm an ambassador for. Unlike previous events, which I managed alone, I worked with a fellow business owner. The goal was to bring together ambitious businesses for a day of learning and networking. We secured keynote speakers and sponsors. Fifty-five people attended, with tickets selling out in 14 days.

5. Eight book launches. Each of my book launches has reached full capacity with every attendee (apart from family!) buying a copy of my book. Venues have varied from bookshops to a local pub, my home, and a conference centre. The number of participants at each launch has ranged from 35 to 120.

For My Client's Businesses

1. Early morning networking events, featuring a marketing masterclass at each to attract bookings. One such event was for an accountancy practice with several branches. Out of 100 people who confirmed their attendance, 84 showed up, comprising existing clients, prospects, and introducers. I delivered my branding masterclass on this occasion.

2. A luncheon club for the same client with the aim of building relationships with key people in the local business community. We invited small business owners and professional introducers, such as financial advisers and bank managers. Hosting an informal luncheon group at a local hotel was the perfect way to establish relationships with every attendee.

3. Online marketing mastermind group. My client, a global brand, wanted their distributors to be more effective at marketing their products. With distributors in 40 countries, hosting an online group was the only option. Attendance at these events ranged from excellent to mediocre, which we expected due to the differing levels of commitment and the varying time zones. We achieved the objective of getting distributors to invest more time in their marketing and sales, and secured a healthy sign-up for my client's in-person conference. It reached capacity, with some attendees travelling thousands of miles. Being able to promote the conference in the run-up to it helped build anticipation and excitement.

4. Media meet-ups. I've arranged several of these, sometimes at a client's premises, but mostly on their exhibition stand. Exhibitions are ideal for reaching out to journalists and editors, especially those who are hard to reach, as most media professionals attend exhibitions relevant to their sector. I've arranged invite-only breakfast events before the show opens, where the format has been to offer a light breakfast before a few speakers share topical insights. I've also arranged informal media drop-ins on a client's stand

with pre-agreed times. Most of the invited journalists and editors have attended, and it has always led to substantial free coverage.

You're Hooked! Where Do You Start?

The following process is what I follow for every event, no matter how small, whether it's an evening masterclass with me as the only speaker, or a full-day conference with a roster of speakers, networking sessions, and breakout seminars. To bring the tips to life, I've used the case study of the non-profit conference I was referring to earlier. I named it Brilliant and Bold (BAB). I've also included the flyer which promoted the event.

- What are your goals?

- Who do you want to invite?

- What will make your event magnetic to delegates and speakers?

- What will make your event appealing to sponsors?

- What type of venue are you looking for?

- What are the maximum number of tickets you can sell?

- How will you create a demand for tickets before they go on sale?

- Is social media the main player or background support?

BRILLIANT & BOLD

An exciting non-profit conference for small business owners looking to scale up, with practical, actionable tips from world class speakers.

Wednesday 24th September 2025
9.30am - 2.45pm

with optional informal networking until 3.30pm
at Horsham Cricket Club, Cricketfield Road RH12 1TE

Are you looking to grow your business on a shoestring budget?

If so, this event is for you. And you'll be supporting two local charities – **Ten Little Toes Baby Bank** and **Moonstones Domestic Abuse Support**.

Every penny from ticket sales will go to charity.

Only 50 tickets available at the early bird price of £35 rising to £50 from July 31st

FIND OUT ABOUT THE SPEAKERS

The speakers...

Our renowned speakers are giving their expertise and time at no charge so we can raise as much money as possible. Tune into their top tips on how you can build your business and boost your profile.

International bestselling marketing author
Dee Blick

Newly published author
Michelle Betts
ByJove Media

Editor of Sussex Exclusive Magazine
Lucy Pitts

ExhibitRate consultancy, founder
Amy Blick

Rachel Martin Coaching
Rachel Martin

Bestselling author and UK Health Radio presenter
Janine Leah

Networking opportunities

Open networking 9.30 - 10am and 2.45 -3.30pm (after final conference session) There will also be a short lunch break of 30 minutes

Event theme

The aim of the day is to inspire, empower and motivate business owners to take their business to the next level. You'll benefit from practical tips and takeouts with masses of experience and expertise on tap.

Brilliant and Bold sponsors

- Architectural Plants, based in Pulborough. You may have seen Guy Watts, Managing Director interviewed on BBC2 recently. Guy is a supporter of many charitable initiatives.

- Lawson & Dawe Properties is a thriving property agency (buying and rentals) in Hove. Lucy Dawe is a longstanding supporter of Ten Little Toes Baby Bank and an avid fundraiser.

- The Marketing Gym, Dee Blick is sponsoring the subsidised venue hire cost, thanks to the generosity of Horsham Cricket Club.

What your ticket includes...

- Thanks to our sponsors, your £35 (early bird) ticket includes Danish pastries, fresh fruit, and hot drinks. A paying bar will open at 12 noon.

- Free pads and pens for every person, courtesy of ByJove Media.

- Parking is free at the venue.

How to secure your early bird ticket

There are only 50 places available. The early bird price of £35 will close on 31st July when the ticket price will rise to £50.

You can buy your ticket at
WeGotTickets.com/BrilliantAndBold
but please do not delay and miss out.

We hope to see you!

BRILLIANT & BOLD SPONSORS

THE MARKETING GYM LTD.   Architectural PLANTS   Lawson & Dawe

What Are Your Goals?

You may want to generate an income, establish yourself as a person of influence, highlight your expertise, build strategic alliances with other people, or even raise money for charity. You can have many objectives. Be clear on them because they will shape your event and subsequent marketing.

The primary aim of BAB was to raise funds for two local charities by bringing ambitious businesses together in a vibrant learning environment. I also wanted to work with other business owners with complementary skills to mine.

Who Do You Want To Invite?

I would imagine that some of the names are included in your personal brand plan as part of your target audience. Compose a list of the actual names, if you can, with their social media and contact details. For BAB, we had a list of small business owners that we knew by name, with most based in a radius of 30 miles from the venue.

What Will Make Your Event Magnetic To Delegates and Speakers?

Making your event magnetic is much easier than you think.

It's about being brilliant at the basics. This means finding generous and engaging speakers willing to share relevant tips and tactics, building in time for networking, and adding a few nice touches such as a competition and decent buffet food – all at a ticket price that won't break the bank. Magnetic speakers don't have to come at a price, especially if your event is non-profit.

If you don't have a speaker budget, could you offer a nice space at your event for speakers to promote their services, latest book, and attendee offers? Let them know you'll promote them in the literature, on your social media, and in any radio interviews. For BAB, we did not have a speaker budget. Luckily, because it was a charity event, speakers were happy to offer their services for free. I secured a media sponsor, which gave additional coverage to our speakers. The interview with Janine Lowe is an example of this. We also promoted speakers in the show flyers, on our social media, and offered a dedicated space at the event for their banner with a small table, allowing them to speak with delegates during the breaks. Making an event magnetic comes down to knowing what will appeal to your audience and then planning a thoughtful, empowering, and informative event. In the leaflet, you can see the billing we gave our speakers. The speaker line-up played a big part in selling tickets, as did the time scheduled for networking.

What Makes Your Event Appealing To Sponsors?

You may have businesses keen to sponsor your event because they want to align with you as a person of influence, and they welcome the opportunity to network with your delegates. For this event, I secured the sponsors with just two emails. We offered them full-page media interviews, social media posts, and a speaking slot on the day. If you want to attract sponsors, create a package that promotes them in the run-up to the event, on the day, and afterwards. It takes minutes to create social posts, thanking your sponsors and including their logos in your promotional literature. You may want sponsors for specific items, such as venue hire costs, refreshments, audio-visual equipment, and the design of literature. Securing sponsors reduces your costs for staging the event, but make sure any package is tempting and that your sponsors align with you, your business, and your delegates.

What Sort of Venue Are You Looking For?

Venues can be expensive, which can significantly increase ticket prices. I start by looking at modern village halls and room hire availability at local sports clubs. They're usually flexible on room hire costs, especially for a non-profit event. The non-negotiables for me are ample free parking on-site, good public transport links nearby, a spacious floor space with decent tables and chairs, power points, nice loos, and facilities for disabled access. If you're overseeing the catering, a suitably equipped on-site kitchen is essential. When people spend several hours at your event, the room they're sitting in must be welcoming and the refreshments plentiful. For BAB, we hired the main function room at our local cricket club. The event manager offered us a reduced day rate, and the caterer provided the sandwiches at no charge. Sponsors covered the cost of the Danish pastries and drinks.

What Are the Maximum Number of Tickets You Can Sell?

The maximum number of tickets depends on the room size and whether delegates are seated in rows or at tables. Speak to the organisers about the maximum number for the room you're hiring and play around with the configuration. For BAB, we sold the maximum of 55 tickets with seating in rows.

How Will You Create a Demand for Tickets Before They Go on Sale?

Creating demand for tickets is the most exciting time. Watching them sell quickly becomes obsessive! Yet it's the area many event organisers stumble on. When tickets are slow to sell, they move into panic mode, giving them away or reducing the price.

The following is my approach to creating a buzz around my events, from piquing curiosity to instilling fear of missing out. I call it my BOSS: Bums on Seats Strategy. Again, this example is from the BAB event.

- Using Facebook and LinkedIn, I sent every person on my VIP list a personal teaser message, as follows. *"Keep 24th September free for the whole day. You're going to love what we've got planned. And you will not want to miss out."* This prompted a flurry of excited messages, which I acknowledged but I resisted the urge to share details about the event.

- Three weeks later, I sent another personal message to the same people: *"At 8am on Friday morning, you'll receive the booking link with the early bird ticket price for a fantastic event we're organising. All profits to charity and some amazing speakers. You are one of just 40 businesses we're sharing this with."* Again, people messaged back with most saying they had saved the date.

- Between 7.30am and 7.55am on the promised day, I sent a personal message to the same people, along with the event flyer and a link to buy tickets. *"Our event will be live from 8am. I hope you will join us at the early bird ticket price of just £35. It is going to be an amazing day supporting two great charities. Message me when you've bought your ticket!"* Every person messaged back to confirm they had bought their ticket or were going to buy it. They also thanked me for thinking of them. The excitement was palpable!

- A few days before opening the event to the public, I sent a personal message to the people on my VIP list who had not yet purchased a ticket, using social media again. *"On Sunday at 6pm, the tickets for our conference will go on sale to everyone. If you haven't yet bought yours, now is the time to do so. I don't want you to miss out on a ticket at the early bird price."* This was not a disingenuous statement. At 6pm, we opened ticket sales to the public on our respective LinkedIn, Facebook, and Instagram profiles.

Did it work?

Every person on our list, except for two people, bought a ticket.

We used social media (Facebook, LinkedIn, and Instagram) to sell the few that remained. We used our social posts to share the names of the businesses that had already bought tickets (with their prior permission). This worked well.

We also found a few extra places after revisiting the venue because some people were keen to attend the event but had not seen our posts.

This event sold out in two weeks.

I have used this BOSS for all my events, including book signings. Naturally, the messages vary to reflect the nature of the event, whether I'm selling tickets or books, for example, but the principle and the time lapse between messages are unaltered. It takes seconds to send personal messages on social media, or an email if a person does not use social media. For BAB, this was the full extent of our marketing efforts. It proves that when you want people to attend your event, sending charming personal messages that pique curiosity and instil FOMO is the best way to sell most of your tickets.

Is Social Media the Main Player or Background Support?

Social media is important in raising awareness of your event, but only after you've aroused the curiosity of the people that you really want to attend, and you've taken them through the process outlined earlier. You may not have to venture beyond your curated list and one-to-one marketing. I've found that even with cold lists, this approach works.

When you start promoting your event on social media beyond your VIP lists, let people know the number of tickets that remain and count down, altering your post with every sale. This will sell the last few tickets. People don't want to miss out.

I've chatted about my BOSS approach with several people who also organise events, and they were of the same opinion. Be relevant, personal, and charming with the people who stand to benefit the most from your event. Start those one-to-one conversations and then leverage other marketing channels. If you give yourself ample time to sell tickets, the reaction to your early bird marketing will indicate the next steps.

How soon should you start promoting your event? For BAB, we started the process at the beginning of June for an event that took place on 24th September. You can, of course, begin much later, but once you've secured your speakers, sponsors, and venue, why not press the green button? People are not averse to booking ahead if your event looks too good to miss.

When You Have Many Tickets To Sell and Your Warm List Is Small

The BOSS approach always works when you know a good number of the potential attendees for your conference. It may be that, as has been the case with my events, a few social media posts are enough to sell the remainder of your tickets. But, what if you're running an event online or in person for several hundred people, many of whom will be new faces?

I encourage you to still leverage the BOSS by targeting your VIP list at early doors so you have time to sell all your tickets. Use their sales to promote your event online, especially if you're targeting specific interest groups, introducers, and using your own social profiles. You may also be targeting members of your professional body or other associations with strong reasons to attend your event. Having several strands of potential sales will help your event sell out quickly.

Your early adopters hold the key to encouraging others to follow suit. Use their reasons for buying a ticket as part of your second phase of marketing. The same techniques – case studies, counting down tickets, a compelling flyer, and a personal video update from you – can be used with great success for the bigger numbers.

Take every opportunity to promote your event on radio, podcasts, webinars, in blogs, and articles. Go back to the previous chapter because your boilerplate is the perfect space to promote your event if you're sharing compelling content. BBC Radio Sussex invited us to speak live on air about the BAB event. However, tickets had sold out several weeks prior to the scheduled interview, so we spoke about the importance of businesses supporting local charities in mutually beneficial ways. The presenter also invited us to return and talk about our next conference.

Don't dismiss the power of those one-to-one conversations with your early adopters to start the ball rolling, regardless of the size of your event. And then take every opportunity you can to promote it. In doing so, you will also be promoting your business and, of course, yourself.

Good luck organising your events. They can truly be one of the most powerful tools in your brand-building kit. I hope you sell every ticket.

Your Takeaways

1. Consider the benefits of hosting your own events, from building influencer status to additional revenue streams.

2. Would organising a media meet-up move you closer to securing substantial coverage for your event, online and in print?

3. Make your event magnetic with great speakers, a warm and welcoming venue, and a powerful theme audiences will love.

4. Sponsors can reduce your costs so create a tempting sponsor package that will make it easy to bring them on board.

5. Once you've booked your venue and speakers, start selling tickets. People will buy, even when your event is months away.

6. When selling tickets, start with your VIP early bird list and use their responses to stimulate sales from cold prospects.

CHAPTER 12

Is There a Book in You?

My different roads to publishing

"Your book opens doors that were previously closed. With a beautifully written and professional looking book in your hands, nowhere is off limits."

W riting a book that displays you as a thought leader is a powerful way to build your personal brand. It conveys your authenticity and brings people closer to you, curious to find out more. A beautifully written, content-rich book opens many doors. If you aim to move from being the *seeker* to the *sought-after*, your book is the ultimate business card.

How do you benefit as an author of a non-fiction book?

- It sets in stone your professional standing as a person of influence.

- It opens doors that were previously closed. With a beautifully written, enticing-looking book in your hands, nowhere is off limits.

- It closes the gap from prospect to paid-up customer.

- It opens new income streams, from public speaking to paid content.

- It adds another layer of credibility to your products and services.

- It can be a legacy of what you've accomplished in an illustrious career.

- It paves the way to altruism and philanthropy. Some authors want to support their favoured charities and causes with their book royalties and speaker fees.

- It can be a credible business blueprint if you're looking to expand your business.

- It elevates you above competitors. You're the exemplar people are taking notice of.

My Publishing Journey

Over the last 18 years, I've written six books (five non-fiction and one fiction), edited two books, and mentored several first-time authors. I've learned valuable lessons along the way and made my fair share of mistakes. If you're considering writing a book, I hope my journey helps you to plan yours.

Powerful Marketing on a Shoestring Budget for Small Businesses

I used a vanity publishing house to produce my book and submitted my final manuscript to them as a Word document.

It cost over £2,000, which, 17 years ago, was steep for what turned out to be a basic level of service. I didn't buy editing services or professional proofreading of the book layout. I received one cover design, which was underwhelming. This decision was made after the account manager informed me that if I wanted multiple designs, I would have to pay for them. I received an average-looking book. The publisher subsequently closed their UK office, so I lost all contact with them. I was unable to purchase any additional copies to sell at signings. Luckily, I had bought enough at the launch. The publisher had loaded my book onto Amazon and made it visible to the international book trade. Because I had not been made exempt from paying US tax when setting up my book on Amazon, my royalties were reduced and it proved impossible to get any money back.

Lessons Learned?

- I should have undertaken due diligence on the publisher and spoken to some of their authors.

- I had mistakenly believed my fee included professional proofreading and several cover designs.

- It was a shock to discover the publisher charged £1.25 for every change I wanted to make to the first proof, including small punctuation changes. And I would only receive two proofs. If I wanted more, I had to pay. I couldn't find any of this in the small print.

My Advice

- Scrutinise the small print before signing up. What's excluded is as important as what's included. Are there limits on the services you would be paying for?

- Find out where the publisher operates from, how long they've been in business, and how they'll support you as your book progresses into production.

The Ultimate Small Business Marketing Book

I was more switched on with this book and used my own cover designer. My husband edited the book as he is meticulous in matters of punctuation and grammar. Between us, we laid out the book. I used a UK-based publisher to allocate the ISBN, consult with the printer, load my book onto Amazon, and secure international distribution. The publisher did not charge for these services. He had a hunch the book was going to be a bestseller, so he would benefit from the royalty share. He was right. We sold thousands of copies worldwide in paperback and e-book format.

I enjoyed the experience because I was in the driving seat, and the publisher was supportive and knowledgeable. At that time, authors didn't have the option of loading their books free of charge onto Amazon Kindle Direct Publishing and buying books directly for their signings, using print-on-demand services from a specialist printer.

Lessons Learned?

I should have paid for a professional layout. I haven't had readers complain, but the homespun layout still jars with me.

My Advice

- Take your time choosing a publisher. Select and pay for the services you need so you can retain control over what you want to manage. Not every publisher offers this flexibility. They may expect you to sign up for a substantial package, so it's important to clarify their conditions and small print upfront.

- Brenda Dempsey, the founder of Book Brilliance Publishing, is an ethical publisher who will happily walk you through the process and your options without asking you to sign up. I chose Book Brilliance Publishing to produce *You're the Best!* I worked with Brenda and her team on a partnership basis, which suited me. They were as meticulous as I am.

- Speak to other authors about their publishers, then draw up your shortlist.

The Ultimate Small Business Marketing Book (Chinese Edition)

CITIC Publishing, based in China, approached me with a contract to buy the rights to translate the book into

Chinese. They found my book on Amazon UK, read the reviews, and wanted to translate it, on the basis it would appeal to small business owners in China. Within two years, the book was available in bookstores in China and online. The production process was lengthy, and the publisher produced many cover designs. The important part I played was maintaining contact with the publishing house and approving cover layouts. It was worth the wait because on the back of this, I secured a significant amount of media coverage in the UK.

Lessons Learned?

Patience! You need plenty of it when your book is being translated. However long you think it will take, multiply it by three. Be prepared to play a long game.

Be courteous and appreciative of your overseas publisher, ensuring that you respect any cultural differences and the different time zones.

My Advice

- Research the publishing house and scrutinise the contract to ensure it is fair to all parties.

- Confirm conversations in writing to keep track of the process and reduce the scope for errors or misunderstanding.

- Ask for several copies of the translated book so you can use them as proof of concept and in your marketing. I received a box of 12 books. This was perfect for the marketing programme I embarked on after publication.

The 15 Essential Marketing Masterclasses for Your Small Business

Following an endorsement from the Chartered Institute of Marketing, Capstone Publishers, an imprint of Wiley, contacted me to offer a publishing deal. Despite them approaching me and giving me free rein on the subject matter, I had to complete a lengthy questionnaire, detailing my background, my following, and how I would promote my book. I had to include a detailed précis of the planned book content, chapter by chapter, and I had to state the number of books I would buy from them for my personal sales.

The team managed every aspect of the book production process, from cover design and layout to editing, proofreading, publishing, international distribution, and launch marketing.

Lessons Learned?

I enjoyed working with a professional publishing team, not to mention the reputational kudos on the back of this. The lack of freedom was occasionally frustrating. If I wanted to make any changes to a chapter, I had to obtain prior approval, and this could take several days. However, I should have spent more time planning the two chapters I subsequently wanted to change so this situation would not have arisen.

I had to plan much further ahead than with my previous books. With a mainstream publishing house, it can take three times as long to publish your book, compared to self-publishing or paying a publisher to produce your book.

My Advice

- For many writers, a paid publishing deal is highly sought after. However, when speaking to the team at Wiley, it was clear they would not have approached me had I not already been an established and successful author.

- You may be offered a book deal with your first book, but it's unlikely. This has no bearing on the quality of your manuscript. Authors who are offered first-time book deals usually have a sizable social following or a large membership base. Some celebrities are also offered first-time book deals because of their popularity, usually with a ghostwriter on hand to ensure the finished book meets the publisher's standards. Don't pin your hopes on a publishing deal and let it halt your progress. As I proved with *The Ultimate Small Business Marketing Book*, you don't need a deal to write a bestseller.

The Ultimate Guide to Writing and Marketing a Bestselling Book

For this book, I followed the same process as *The Ultimate Small Business Marketing Book* by using the same publisher. This time, however, I paid for the book cover, editing, and layout.

Lessons Learned?

- The book was too large and bulky which reduced its appeal and made it expensive to post. Some readers found the book overwhelming. They were right.

- If I had my time again, I would halve the page count and reduce the subject matter. Although this had been my gut instinct, I failed to act on it.

- It was listed in *The Guardian* newspaper's top 10 reads for entrepreneurs, but it did not make a dent in the bestsellers. Great for my ego, less so for book sales!

- I'm pleased to report that in recent years, it has proved popular in filling places at my author workshops. I offer a free copy with every sign-up.

My Advice

Size is everything and you may have several books in you, covering the same subject. Indeed, the trend with non-fiction books seems to be less is more.

The Boutique: A Collection of Nine Short Stories

For this book, I managed most of the production process. I found an excellent editor specialising in fiction and had the cover professionally designed by a local designer. I sold the paperback on Amazon at no cost to me, using Kindle Direct Publishing. My designer and typesetter used the free templates on KDP which worked well. I also had an e-book produced. A publisher uploaded the book to the Nielsen database so I could sell it through bookshops. This strategy meant using a special ISBN (the barcode on the back cover). Amazon provide a free ASIN, which is the equivalent of an ISBN but this is only valid for sales on Amazon. I also had 400 copies produced by a printer to a higher specification than the Amazon paperback. I paid extra for a soft-touch cover and the pages were 100gsm in weight (the standard is 80gsm). Even at this higher specification, the unit cost per book from my printer was still £1 cheaper than the unit cost Amazon KDP quoted for the same book, and at an inferior quality.

Lessons Learned?

Although this was a smooth and enjoyable process, I encountered delays due to the many errors with the professional layout, which was challenging and ultimately delayed the project by several days. I had to remind myself that the road to publishing success can sometimes be fraught, even for an experienced pro like me! The book has only been available for the last few months, so watch this space. I sell it mostly at book signings and writer events.

My Advice

- Talk to a printer that specialises in short-run digital printing for your direct sales. Extra touches that will make your book look and feel premium quality add pennies to the unit cost, but are worth it.

- If you're self-publishing and using professionals for services such as design and layout, ask for samples of their recent work. How long does it take to deliver their service? How many proofs are included in their fee? What is their turnaround for corrections?

If you're a fledgling author, take control of your publishing journey. I understand the allure of a paid publishing deal and why you would want to say yes without thinking twice. If a publisher offers you a deal, talk to them about every facet of the deal, what they expect from you, and vice versa. They might publish your book without offering an advance, and their marketing activities may primarily involve social media posts, with authors frequently responsible for much of the promotion. If you know the details upfront, you'll not be disappointed or surprised at their requests or, indeed, their lack of support further down the line.

If you're paying a publisher to produce your book, again, study the small print and their services. An ethical publisher will not encourage you to buy services you neither need nor can afford.

Don't sign up for marketing services until after your book has been produced. It's much easier to add a service than it is to extricate yourself from one, bought in the first flush of enthusiasm. Will you need to pay for a publisher's marketing support? If you've started talking about your book on social media and promoted it to your target audiences whilst writing it, you may be able to build on this without further help.

In the next chapter, we look at how you can write and produce a book that reflects your authentic and magnetic personal brand.

Your Takeaways

1. A non-fiction book is your best business card, positioning you as a magnetic person of influence, and positively differentiating you from your peers.

2. When choosing a publisher, check the small print to understand what you're getting and any restrictions on their services.

3. Don't be tempted to take on production elements to save money if you have neither the skills nor the time.

4. You don't need a publishing deal to produce an excellent book that sells and that promotes your influencer status.

5. Trust your gut instinct when it comes to certain aspects of your book. You're the one living with it and promoting it.

6. Ask for samples of recent work when assembling your team.

CHAPTER 13

How To Write Your Best Book

Shoestring style with quality front of mind

"Your book should look as though a mainstream publisher has produced it, even if you self-published it. Don't stint on its kerb appeal."

Writing a non-fiction book is an enjoyable, time-consuming, and sometimes challenging process. Increasingly, I'm seeing businesspeople putting pen to paper, often for many of the reasons outlined in the previous chapters. Your book can work wonders in building your reputation and opening the doors that have previously resisted your attempts. It positions you as an authentic and influential person.

However, the simple act of writing and publishing a book does not automatically confer a magical brand-building status, with your book leading from the front as a magnet for new business and stellar connections.

It's not enough to write a mediocre book in the hope that it will land with someone somewhere. Your book must be the best book you're capable of writing. And it must look the part. I've seen books that have slipped through the radar of an editor and a designer. The spelling mistakes and clumsy grammar are the consequence of the author's sprint to the finish line. Sometimes, the content bears no trace of the author's business DNA. It fails to highlight their expertise and experience. It becomes yet another book destined to sink into obscurity. As for the cover, the author has taken it upon themselves to add 'designer' to their skill set when they should have used a professional.

Something that is alarmingly rearing its head today is the idea that an author can write a book without breaking a sweat. I recently saw a manuscript that was a tribute to ChatGPT rather than the author's talent. He had clearly taken shortcuts and his generic book was proof of this. He hadn't realised he was treating his book like a commodity, aiming to finish it quickly with minimal effort. He had attended a free seminar on how to write a book without writing a word of it. The gist was that he should feed his ideas into ChatGPT, train it to recognise his style, and then simply top and tail the content.

Hey presto, a star is born!

Until another book looking suspiciously similar enters the fray.

So if you want to write a compelling book, one that you're proud to showcase as a dazzling example of your authentic and magnetic personal brand, and one that really does capture your unique voice and experience, where do you start?

These tips will help you craft your best book.

My Nine Non-Negotiables

1. Determine your Whys.

2. Find your readers and their sweet spot.

3. Gather your content. And plan your chapters.

4. Include contributors if they add value.

5. Be available to write.

6. Use an editor.

7. Ensure you get a professional, appealing, and inclusive layout.

8. Have a professionally designed, enticing cover.

9. The price must be right.

1. **Determine your Whys.** Why do you want to write a book? If you have several answers to this question, you're on promising ground, because our reasons help us reach the finishing line with a completed book. Are your 'Whys' of sufficient gravitas to motivate you to write, even when you're knee-deep in running your business? Write down your 'Whys' and keep them close to hand – time to return to Chapters 6 and 7.

2. **Find your readers and their sweet spot.** When I run workshops for authors, this is the exercise many find the most challenging. Yet they will declare it the most satisfying once they've started thinking in

depth about their readers beyond vague descriptions that provide little insight when the time for targeting arrives. This exercise is the same when you're evaluating your marketing strategy and creating your personal brand plan. I would imagine that some of your reader groups will appear in these.

Fundamentally, you're writing a book that will appeal to people that will really enjoy reading it and recommending it.

You may have several groups of readers. Make a note of each one and, beside the name, jot down what they're likely to want from your book. This will help at the content planning stage and, of course, with the subsequent marketing.

For example, I mentored first-time author Rachael Sadler to write *Life After Lottie*. Rachael's book recounts the journey she undertook after losing her dog, Lottie. It encompasses her experiences working as a volunteer at Soi Dog Foundation in Thailand. Rachael's 'why' in writing her book was threefold. She wanted to reach out to pet owners experiencing the grief of losing their dog to show them they were not alone. She also wanted to raise awareness of the remarkable work of Soi Dog Foundation. Finally, she wanted to fundraise for the Foundation. This experience helped Rachael to plan her chapters in detail. She included several volunteer case studies so that readers could learn more about the heart-warming work of the Foundation. John Dalley MBE, President and co-founder of Soi Dog Foundation, wrote the foreword to her book. With her 'why' front of mind, Rachael began to identify her readers. This included a fundraising ball for Soi Dog Foundation, an event that many volunteers attend. Rachael was offered a signing spot in the venue's foyer. There is also a shop that fundraises for the Foundation, and it now stocks Rachael's book. Visitors to the shop are dog lovers and supporters. Rachael is also contacting groups of dog lovers online through social media and special membership groups.

I recently ran a workshop for authors at a popular local book festival, Billilit. One attendee told me she was finding it hard to identify her target readers, beyond the fact that her book would appeal to women with a love of historical fiction. After this simple exercise, she had a list of museums she could target that were visited by her audience, plus several online groups comprising women that would be interested in her book's subject matter. Spending time on her ideal readers, including where to find them, had given her enough information to form a plan.

Consider…

- Where do your readers gather?

- Do they meet online and/or in person?

- Do they belong to groups and forums?

- Can you identify the membership associations, special interest groups, professional associations, and buying groups they belong to?

- Which exhibitions and events are they likely to attend?

- Which magazines, newsletters, and special interest publications are they likely to read?

- What will make your book appealing to them?

3. **Gather your content. And plan your chapters**. If you're writing a book as the ultimate expression of your expertise and knowledge, you will have content that can be repurposed, reused, and rewritten. For example, training handouts, blogs, articles, videos, manuals, brochures, magazines, tips, podcast recordings, transcripts of keynote talks, and webinars. Gather these strands into a central point so you can decide what you're going to use and where to use it. Can you share case studies and client stories to underpin your subject matter and bring the narrative to life? What are the extras you can bring to your book by way of engaging content? This is the content that will elicit a "Wow!" and that will lead to great reviews and recommendations.

Don't skimp on this stage.

It could take several weeks. Keep gathering, right up to the last chapter. You'll be inspired as you go about your daily business, so be ready to capture ideas at any time. I travel everywhere with a writing pad and several pens. I am also known for writing on napkins and till receipts.

Sketch out the structure of each chapter; what it must include and why. Can you see a consistent approach evolving? Will you summarise your chapters so time-pressed readers can grasp the key points? How will you maintain a natural flow from one chapter to the next, despite differing subject matter? I spend a few months on this and, up to the last minute, I am processing ideas.

4. **Include contributors if they add value**. I've always included contributors in my non-fiction books. Contributors can underpin some of your content; they can augment it, and they can add a new dimension. Their inclusion can enable you to paint a more detailed picture for readers. Be clear on the reasons for including contributors, and choose people who are not only subject matter experts in their field, but they also complement your personal brand and your business brand. They must align with your values and authenticity. When asking for their content, provide a brief description, including the word count, submission date, and what you're looking for. Make sure they agree to your planned book promotions. Tell them not to reproduce the content they've written for your book without your prior permission. This lack of clarity happened to me once. It was annoying because the contributor published the material he'd written for my book a few weeks before its launch.

5. **Be available to write.** You may be capable of writing for just 30 minutes a day and out pops the most beautiful manuscript. If this is you, please share your secret!

I must schedule writing time into my work and life plan for the week ahead. And I write for a living. So if you can get into the habit of blocking out time to write with your mobile out of sight, you'll make real progress. The more you write, the easier it becomes. Stay hydrated or you'll tire prematurely.

6. **Use an editor.** An editor is crucial regardless of the genre of your book. Before handing your completed manuscript to your editor, make sure you've read it several times, red pen close to hand. You can root out the obvious inconsistencies, tighten up on some descriptions, expand on others, and gain a deeper understanding of your book. I read through my final manuscripts at least 10 times before releasing them to my editor. I want their focus to be on polishing my prose, not rolling up their sleeves and radically overhauling it.

Editors provide several tiers of service, starting with the basics – a good first run of your book, weeding out errors, poor punctuation, sloppy grammar, and inconsistencies. I opt for this level of editing. This decision leads to a comprehensive appraisal of your book, followed by significant changes to your text and large-scale rewording. Before appointing an editor, send your first completed, self-edited chapter to the one that appeals to you.

Then wait for their feedback.

Look upon your editor as your closest book buddy. It's their job to ensure that your book is polished to near perfection, so let them do their job.

How to choose an editor?

You'll find editors with impressive portfolios on freelancer sites and sites such as LinkedIn. Choose one with experience in non-fiction books.

For the editing of this book, I worked with Brenda Dempsey, founder of Book Brilliance Publishing and Zara Thatcher, a Professional Member of the Chartered Institute of Editing and Proofreading (CIEP). I also recommend Olivia Eisinger, an experienced freelance editor and proofreader, who is also a member of the CIEP.

Lucy Pitts is an experienced editor and author. You may recall her strapline from Chapter 3: she is the disruptive copywriter. When I asked her to write a few lines for me, explaining the need for an editor, she sent the following:

"Writing a non-fiction book is an opportunity to elevate your brand and position you as a thought leader. It's also a labour of love. To make sure it's pitch-perfect, you'll need the help of an editorial eye. Working with your preferred writing style, Lucy can work with you, chapter by chapter, making sure you have the appropriate structure, cadence, and message, or by providing editorial input at the end, to give your book the necessary finishing polish."

Don't be tempted to forego the skills of an editor. The last thing you want is an eagle-eyed reader pointing errors out when they're reviewing your book because they will!

7. **Ensure you get a professional, appealing, and inclusive layout.** Your book should be visually appealing and easy to read. Many books still have pages crammed with text where the publisher or author aimed to reduce production costs by minimising the page count. This decision is a false economy. When a person browses your book online, if the sample pages are packed with unreadable text, they're unlikely to move past the first point. Lay out your manuscript as you would like to read it, with space, stand-out sentences, and small paragraphs. Then leave the task to the professional typesetter so they have a good idea of what you're looking for.

The following layout suggestions of a book refers to the additional pages that are easy to overlook if you're self-publishing. Follow this structure and a reader will be unable to tell the difference between your self-published book and one produced by a mainstream publisher.

Front matter includes the content of your book that appears before the first chapter, or the main body text. Front matter elements usually appear in this order:

1. Half title page

2. Title page

3. Copyright

4. Reviews and praise

5. Dedication

6. Table of contents

7. Foreword

8. Introduction

Body matter includes all content between the front and back matter. This typically contains all part pages and chapters.

Back matter includes all content that appears after the last chapter, or at the end of the main body of the text. Back matter sections typically include references and the author acknowledgements.

The person laying out your book will be familiar with the placement of these pages; for example, what appears on a right-hand page and what appears on a left-hand page. It is your job to ensure this content is in the correct order for layout, and then let your layout professional take over.

Your book should look as though a publisher has professionally produced it, even if, in fact, you have self-published it. Don't stint on its kerb appeal. My first fiction book, *The Boutique*, was self-published. This did not stop my local Waterstones bookshop inviting me to a signing and talk. Afterwards, *The Boutique* was on their shelves, at home with their biggest fiction titles. Make sure your book has the same status.

8. **Have a professionally designed, enticing cover.** Your cover is the shop window of your book. Make sure yours is eye-catching, relevant, and interesting to readers. Don't cut corners by designing the cover yourself using stock images and generic text. Use a professional designer and brief them so they understand your target readers, the content of your book, the genre, what you're looking for, and any small details. When I'm at this stage, I give my designer creative freedom, albeit within the parameters of my detailed brief.

So what should a magnetic cover include?

- Testimonial on the front or back, ideally from a person of influence and clearly connected to the subject matter of your book.

- Title and subtitle, with the latter explaining why your book is a must-read.

- On the back cover, a summary of your book, complete with several hooks, painting a picture of what's inside so readers want to dive in and discover more.

- Your picture, accompanied by a few words so that readers can form a connection and put a face to the name.

- Your ISBN (ASIN if you're restricting online sales to Amazon and are not looking to distribute to the broader book trade).

- Your book's retail price (RRP).

Don't be tempted to cram the back cover with text. Paint a compelling picture in 100 words.

Your designer must know the size of your book. I used Amazon's royalty calculator on Kindle Direct Publishing to determine the size of *The Boutique*. My designer also used their free design templates.

9. **The price must be right.** If you're planning to sell your book online through distributors such as Amazon, they take a whopping 60% of the cover price of your book. So if your book retails at £15, £9 goes to the reseller. This leaves you with £6 from which you must deduct the cost of producing your book. What's left behind is your royalty. The number of pages will influence the unit cost of producing your book, as will any colour images inside and special finishes on the cover, such as foil blocking, embossing, or a soft touch. You can make your book so expensive to produce that there is no wiggle room for any royalty after all expenses have been deducted. If you're collaborating with a publisher to set up international distribution of your book, you will have to pay for shipping costs and setup fees unless you've been offered a publishing deal. For a non-fiction book, you can charge more than for a fiction book of a similar size. I arrived at the RRP for *You're the Best!* by weighing up all these factors and considering the prices of other books in the same category.

Paper, Pixels, or Both?

Something I wanted to touch on this chapter is whether you publish your book in paperback, e-book, or both. I use both formats. It comes down to what you think readers will buy. Whilst you make the most margin by selling your paperback books directly, you may have a bestseller on your hands through e-book sales alone. The cost of formatting your e-book is inexpensive because it is based on the paperback format. You will, however, need a separate ISBN for it, which you can buy online.

I hope you've found these tips useful. Use them to inspire your book and build your magnetic personal brand.

Your Takeaways

1. Make your book the best book you're capable of writing and producing.

2. ChatGPT is no substitute for writing a book. It requires authenticity, not corner cutting.

3. Establish your non-negotiables at the outset to guide you at every stage of your book's journey.

4. Be clear about your target readers, where you'll find them, and why they'll love your book.

5. Content gathering and establishing chapter structure and flow are crucial.

6. Your editor, layout professional, and cover designer are three of your book's best allies. Don't be tempted to go it alone.

7. Price your book to cover production costs, reseller margin, royalties, and the price of similar books in the category.

Some Final Words From Dee

You've reached the end of my book. I hope you're brimming with ideas, along with a to-do list and a personal brand plan that excites you and fills you with optimism. In moments of doubt, remind yourself that you're more than good enough to succeed, and that the road ahead is full of untapped potential. Celebrate the small wins because they build momentum and self-trust, and aim for progress, not perfection. Being curious, generous, and leading with purpose and passion will take you far.

Stand in your circle of power as a relatable, authentic, and magnetic person of influence, and enjoy every step of the journey. Share your success with others and watch your personal brand flourish.

Life is short and precious. Make the most of yours, just as I have.

I'd love to know how you get on. You can contact me on Facebook and LinkedIn or dee@themarketinggym.org

Dee Blick

The Experts

Amy Blick FCIPD

I'm the founder of exhilHRate Ltd. I help ambitious businesses drive performance, engagement, and profit through smart, strategic people management. From leadership development and performance frameworks to tricky ER – if it's about your people, I make it impactful and commercially sharp. I've grown teams from the inside and so understand fast-paced businesses. Clients say I challenge, energise, and deliver with heart, hustle, and commercial sense. Clients tend to be high-growth, value-led businesses that care about their people and want to scale smart. Think law firms, forward-thinking accountants, and growing SMEs looking for more than just policies. They want people strategies that power commercials and drive the business forward. You can connect with me through many channels.

Amy@exhilHRate.co.uk

LinkedIn: www.linkedin.com/in/amy-blick-exhilhrate/

Instagram: www.instagram.com/exhilhrate

Upcoming Training & Events: www.eventbrite.co.uk/o/exhilhrate-53528544143

Debbie Green

I'm the founder of Wishfish Coaching & Development and co-host of the Secrets from a Coach podcast. As an award-winning ICF accredited life coach, I'm all about helping people build confidence, boost wellbeing, and navigate life's twists and turns with a positive mindset and self-belief. Whether I'm coaching one-on-one, running leadership workshops, or recording our podcast (now with over 50,000 downloads!), I'm passionate about helping others thrive. After a serious car accident in 2010, I truly learned the power of resilience. I now use that experience to inspire others to take care of themselves and go after what they really want. I believe anything is possible with the right attitude, a little encouragement, and a healthy dose of humour along the way.

Call me on 07896 998137, or email info@wishfish.org.uk

Ted Gooda

Ted is a poet, playwright, and ghostwriter based in Sussex. Her debut pamphlet *Silence & Selvedge* was published in 2024, and her poems have appeared in *Wildfire Words*, *Frosted Fire*, *Sentinel*, *The Cannon's Mouth*, *The Dawntreader*, and others. Her fourth play, *Mannequim*, premièred at the Brighton Fringe Festival in 2025. She ghostwrites a *Sunday Times* top 10 bestselling series with Mirror Books, writing as Theresa McEvoy. Ted also coordinates several literary festivals across the South of England, runs writing workshops, and is chair of West Sussex Writers.

You can contact her via www.theresagooda.co.uk

Stefan Thomas

Stefan is the bestselling author of *Business Networking for Dummies* as well as Amazon bestsellers *Instant Networking* and *Win the Room*. He is an exceptionally popular keynote speaker and MC, known for leaving his audiences not only amused but with actionable tactics they can take away and use straight away. Many audience members have commented publicly that they made sales immediately after leaving one of Stefan's events and implementing his advice. As a result, Stefan speaks for the likes of BT, Telecom Plus Plc, Lloyds Bank, The Chartered Institute of Management Accountants, The Loo of the Year Awards, and many more.

You can connect with Stefan at www.stefanthomas.biz – or find him down the front of one of the many punk gigs he still attends!

Michelle Betts

Michelle is the founder of ByJove Media, an award-winning strategic social media consultancy helping small businesses and organisations turn likes into lasting impressions. She combines years of corporate experience with proven social media know-how, offering a no-nonsense, results-driven approach. Her Power Hours and Audits are highly valued by clients looking for practical advice they can act on straight away. Michelle is known for her social media expertise and building content strategies that work. Clients include retailers, consultancy firms, and purpose-led brands. Alongside her social media agency work, she recently published her debut novel *Smoke and Mirrors* under the pen name Michelle Plater. It is an emotionally immersive, celebrity romance, available on Amazon.

Follow her on Instagram: @ByJoveMedia / @ByJoveBooks.

David Beeney

David enjoyed a successful 30-year career in the world of media. But, during that time, he was hiding something. Eventually in 2016, he found the courage to open up about the most significant struggle of his life: his mental health. A secret battle with panic attacks meant years of torment and angst. David's decision to break his silence was the most transformative moment of his life. Today, David's business, Breaking the Silence, is regarded as one of the world's leading advisors on mental health in the workplace. He has worked with leading global brands including HSBC, McDonald's, Mercedes, and Google. David is listed in the top 101 global influencers and, in 2024, he published his highly acclaimed book, *Breaking the Silence.*

His website address is www.breakingthesilence.co.uk

Debbie Gilbert

Debbie is the powerhouse behind Viva Business Group which encompasses Viva Business Support, Businesswomen UnLtd, and The Best Businesswomen Awards.

A multi-award-winning entrepreneur and marketing expert, Debbie has won 11 business awards and passionately champions others through her work. She is the author of *The Successful Mumpreneur*, a practical guide for women balancing business and family, and host of The Business Awards Show podcast, where she shares insights from inspiring award-winning entrepreneurs and other award organisers. Her expertise, authenticity, and tireless support of women in business have earned her a stellar reputation and loyal following. Whether she's mentoring start-ups, running award-winning networking events, or celebrating excellence through her awards programme, Debbie is known for helping others shine.

Connect on LinkedIn: www.linkedin.com/in/debgilbert

Further Reading and Resources

Books Mentioned in the Text

Susan Jeffers, *Feel the Fear and Do It Anyway*, Ebury Press, 2007

Deepak Chopra, *The Seven Spiritual Laws of Success*, Bantam Press, 1996

David Beeney, *Breaking the Silence*, Filament Publishing, 2024

Stefan Thomas, *Business Networking for Dummies*, For Dummies, 2014

Philip Kotler, Waldemar Pfoertsch, *Ingredient Branding: Making the Invisible Visible*, Springer, 2010

Janine Lowe, *Feng Shui Your Way to Abundance*, O-Books, 2024

Rachael Sadler, *Life After Lottie*, Aliciam Books, 2025

Other Books

Professor Steve Peters, *The Chimp Paradox*, Vermilion, 2012

Dr Danny Penman, Vidyamala Burch, *Mindfulness for Health*, Piatkus, 2013

Pearl Letlotlo Olesitse, *The Path of Pearl*, Book Brilliance Publishing, 2025

Dale Carnegie, *How to Win Friends and Influence People*, Simon & Schuster, 1936

Dorothy Carnegie, *The Quick and Easy Way to Effective Speaking*, Association Press, 1962

David Ogilvy, *Ogilvy on Advertising*, Welbeck Publishing, 2007

Brenda Dempsey, *Voices of Women: Creating Ripples of Brilliance*, Book Brilliance Publishing, 2024

Brad Burton, *Life. Business: Just Got Easier*, Capstone, 2013

Magazines

Health Triangle Magazine: ukhealthradio.com/magazine

Other Contributors' Websites

Lucy Pitts, Editor: www.sussexexclusive.com

Mike Schlup, Kalimex: www.kalimex.co.uk

Alan and Jeanette Landale, AJ Fleetcare: www.ajfleetcare.co.uk

Guy Watts, Architectural Plants:
www.architecturalplants.com

Kirstie Betts, Pied A Terre Adventures:
www.patadventures.com

Katie Wellman, Make Room to Breathe:
www.makeroomtobreathe.co.uk

Angus Grady: www.linkedin.com/in/angusgrady

Mike Yorke: www.horshamgolf.co.uk

Useful Organisations

The Chartered Institute of Marketing: www.cim.co.uk

FSB (Federation of Small Business): www.fsb.org.uk

Toastmasters International: www.toastmasters.org

Networking Groups

Business Networking International: www.bni.co.uk

1230 TWC (Founder: Jackie Groundsell):1230.co.uk

Businesswomen UnLtd (Founder: Debbie Gilbert):
businesswomenunltd.co.uk

The Great British Business Show:
www.greatbritishbusinessshow.co.uk

Women's Institute: www.thewi.org.uk

Acknowledgements

There are many special people I owe a debt of gratitude to.

Firstly, I must thank my content contributors, an eclectic group of talented, authentic, and magnetic people. They are: Stefan Thomas, Michelle Betts, Debbie Gilbert, Amy Blick, Debbie Green, David Beeney, and Ted Gooda.

For my cover design, I thank the super talented Melanie Tilly. Melanie also designed the cover for *The Ultimate Small Business Marketing Book*. It was special to be working with her again.

A big thank you to Brenda Dempsey, the founder of Book Brilliance Publishing, the publisher of *You're the Best!* It was an incredible experience to be working with such a talented, organised, proactive, and ethical publisher.

Thanks to Zara Thatcher, who not only proofed every page of my book with an unerring eye for every detail, but was also the talent behind the layout of the paperback. Thanks also to Olivia Eisinger for her expert editorial support.

On the family front, special thanks go to my wonderful husband Malcolm, and my little brother Drew, who has the biggest heart.

Finally, I can't thank you enough for buying *You're the Best!* I hope you've enjoyed reading it as much as I've enjoyed writing it.

Use it as your springboard to success.

With gratitude,

Dee X

dee@themarketinggym.org

www.linkedin.com/in/creativemarketer

www.facebook.com/dee.blick

www.ingramcontent.com/pod-product-compliance
Lightning Source LLC
Chambersburg PA
CBHW071332210326
41597CB00015B/1424